KEEP THE CALL

LEADING THE CONGREGATION WITHOUT LOSING YOUR SOUL

JILL Y. CRAINSHAW

ABINGDON PRESS
Nashville

KEEP THE CALL: LEADING THE CONGREGATION
WITHOUT LOSING YOUR SOUL

Copyright © 2007 by Abingdon Press

All rights reserved.

This book is printed on acid-free paper.

Library of Congress Cataloging-in-Publication Data

Crainshaw, Jill Y., 1962-

　Keep the call : leading the congregation without losing your soul / Jill Y. Crainshaw.

　　p. cm.

　Includes bibliographical references.

　ISBN-13: 978-0-687-64145-1 (binding: pbk., adhesive perfect : alk. paper)

　1. Pastoral theology.　2. Clergy—Appointment, call, and election.　I. Title.

　BV4011.3.C73 2007

　253—dc22

2006028430

07 08 09 10 11 12 13 14 15 16—10 9 8 7 6 5 4 3 2 1

MANUFACTURED IN THE UNITED STATES OF AMERICA

Contents

Acknowledgments

This book grows out of sustained conversations with many people who have encouraged me to "keep the call." My students at the Wake Forest University Divinity School have been vital to the creation of this manuscript. They consistently challenge, inspire, and encourage my work. The Wake Forest University Divinity School faculty and staff have been consistently supportive and encouraging. Colleagues who have been directly helpful in reading portions of the manuscript include Mark Jensen, and Bill Leonard (Dean of the Wake Forest University Divinity School). I also express gratitude to my friend and former teaching partner, Brad Braxton, whose passion for ministry and theological education often sparked ideas and stirred convictions central to the manuscript. Brian Graves graduated from Wake Forest University Divinity School in 2006. Without his careful research and bibliographic expertise, this manuscript might still be on my desk waiting for final editing. Special thanks goes to my colleagues Melissa Clodfelter and Dave Odom, friends and vocational formation partners whose tireless listening and asking questions regularly propelled me forward with this project. Similarly, I thank Ginny Simpson who provided an open door, good coffee, and many hours of valuable coaching as I wrote and re-wrote chapters of the manuscript. Finally, I am deeply grateful to Sheila Hunter, piano technician and musical *compañera*, who not only stirred insights about piano strings and soundboards (which are a part of the manuscript) but who also reminds me regularly about life tunings and ministry. *Keep the Call* is dedicated to the memory of my dad, Jerry, and in honor of my mother, Sarah, who let me know in many ways the joyful meanings of being created in the image and sound of God.

Introduction

The fifty-year anniversary celebration echoed with memories of days gone by. Birthed in the middle of the twentieth century, in a growing suburb, Southside Avenue Church quickly became a vital part of the neighborhood. Young professionals bought and built homes in the community. They brought their ideas, visions, and financial resources with them to worship. By 1960, Southside Avenue Church bulged at the seams with over two hundred worshipers, and members imagined one day hearing the sound of nails being pounded into the rafters of a new sanctuary.

By contrast, the fifty-seven voices lifted in prayer and singing on that anniversary Sunday morning in 2002 echoed hollowly in a building now noticeably too big and regrettably underutilized. The cutting of the fiftieth-anniversary cake was a sharp reminder. Too much of what was celebrated was in the past. Not enough anticipated a thriving future. Southside Avenue Church was not the same congregation that years earlier contributed energy, leadership, and spiritual vitality to the neighborhood.

For many years, Southside Avenue Church stood as a vibrant and respected symbol of Christian faith in the community. But the Southside neighborhood has changed. Most houses within a mile of Southside Avenue Church are now rental properties, and first-generation immigrants, primarily from Mexico, populate over half of these properties. New signs have appeared outside shops and stores up and down the streets near the church. The brightly colored Spanish words on these signs proclaim a reality. The Southside neighborhood story is very different today than it was fifty years ago.

Southside Avenue Church's story is also very different today. For example, attendance decreases each year as younger members migrate to other churches. The church building and membership are aging. Some members want to remodel the building. Others want to relocate. The current budget will support neither of these ideas.

Eight months ago, Andrea was called to be Southside Avenue Church's sixth pastoral leader. The church's first four pastoral leaders enjoyed tenures of more than ten years each. By contrast, the pastoral leader just prior to Andrea departed after only twenty-four months. The primary cause was the sharp difference between congregational expectations and the pastoral leader's strategies for renewal in a changing neighborhood.

With the ink still damp on her master of divinity diploma, Andrea eagerly anticipated making connections between her story and Southside Avenue's story. Viewed through the windows of her multicultural ministry classroom, Southside Avenue looked like a perfect place for Andrea to live out her pastoral call. A church like Southside Avenue, Andrea thought, has an ideal opportunity to show hospitality to and share God's grace with neighborhood newcomers.

Andrea soon learned that weaving her vocational story together with Southside Avenue's story was going to be hard work. Though they yearn for renewal, many members of Southside Avenue are nevertheless hesitant to reach out to their new neighbors. Most members now live five or six miles from the church. The Spanish-speaking Southside neighborhood is unfamiliar territory.

Uncertain what steps to take next, many in the congregation are looking to the church's more vibrant past. That is why more than a few words spoken around the anniversary feast tables were seasoned with longing: "I don't understand why people don't come to church anymore." "This neighborhood just isn't like it used to be." "What happened to the days when the choir was filled with teenagers?" The only story many church members seem able to hear is the story of the past, a story distorted by change and nostalgia.

Even so, one characteristic that drew Andrea to Southside Avenue Church has endured neighborhood change and congregational conflict. Over the years, the people of Southside Avenue have nurtured a steady belief in God's presence and grace. Each time Andrea stands behind the pulpit for a funeral service, she sees this belief reflected in members' faces. She glimpses those places deep in the soul of the congregation where faith and hope reside.

Likewise, when members pass the peace during Sunday morning worship, Andrea knows she is witnessing more than a weekly ritual. People in this congregation really care about one another. Andrea senses in this spirit of care hope for future congregational health and vitality.

Southside Avenue Church's anniversary celebration marked an important congregational milestone. But tones of sadness dulled the celebration's joyous proclamations. Several denominational consultants were present, congratulating church members but also hinting at possible partnerships with other small congregations.

Older members raised their eyebrows in skepticism. Denominational connections were not considered important in the 1960s and 1970s when the church was thriving. Even now, most members still prefer "to stay out of all of that denominational business." Denominational fingerprints on their congregational identity are deemed intrusive.

A few weeks after the anniversary celebration, Andrea and the governing council met to consider their financial situation. The church would not make its budget this year. Andrea longed for church members to imagine celebrating a "fiesta" the next year along with an "anniversary party" or breaking a piñata along with cutting the cake. But she was unsure how to lead church members toward such a change: "How can I lead Southside Avenue Church to reclaim and renew its identity as a sacred place where all people can find hospitality and experience God's grace? Is there a model for ministry that will really work for me and my congregation?"

Modeling Ministry: A Search for What Really Works

Keep the Call explores three dimensions of ministry: ministry as proclamation, ministry as formation, and ministry as transformation. These dimensions are important resources for congregations and pastoral leaders who seek ministry models that really work.

Several questions guide this search for effective ministry models:

- What is the role of congregations in changing communities?
- What is the key to effective ministry in changing communities?
- How can pastoral leaders cultivate their deepest callings and passions while leading congregations whose identities are in transition?

Andrea and Southside Avenue Church are not alone in facing these questions. Many pastoral leaders and congregations of various sizes and demographics wrestle with ministerial identity crises.

Ministry *models* give congregations frameworks for addressing questions of identity, values, and purpose. In recent years, congregations and pastoral leaders have used models from a variety of theoretical, religious, and secular perspectives. Many of these models focus on important aspects of ministry and leadership. But some are not strongly enough linked to ministry's spiritual and theological dimensions.[1] Other models lack clear communal dimensions. Robust theological *and* communal dimensions are essential if congregations are to proclaim God's grace effectively in diverse neighborhoods and communities.

Keep the Call falls into three sections. Each section explores one of the dimensions of ministry mentioned above. Each dimension is deemed essential as congregations and pastoral leaders respond to God's call to be the church in today's world.

Ministry as proclamation is the focus of the first section. Healthy and effective ministry involves hearing God's voice (vocation), discerning one's own voice (spiritual formation), and learning to use that voice to proclaim the gospel both within the community and to the world (prophetic witness). Ministry as proclamation is not the responsibility of a congregation's pastoral leader alone. Southside Avenue Church, *as a congregation*, is called to proclaim something true and reliable about God within the Southside neighborhood.

Ministry as formation is the focus of the second section. As narrative theologians have told us, conversion into and within the life of the church happens when individuals hear their own stories within God's story and embrace God's story in Christ as their own. Weaving together human and divine stories is a lifelong process and requires congregational leaders who both proclaim and embody Christ's story in their own lives. Through this work of formation, congregations provide consistency, continuity, and community to people seeking roots for chaotic lives.

Ministry as transformation is the focus of the third section of the book. Pastoral leaders struggle to do their work somewhere between the call to creativity and transformation on the one hand, and the day-to-day administrative requirements of organizational life on the other. Faithful leadership is characterized by the ability to work within the structures and demands of institutional life while calling congregations to their vocations of leadership in the world. Vocations of public leadership demand congregational resilience and willingness to change. Southside Avenue Church's call to transformation demands an intentional partnership between administration, imagination, and leadership.

Why a Different Approach Is Needed

The Southside Avenue Church council's tense discussion about another budget shortfall is also about how the church will imagine its future. Thus, wistful stories about the past as well as possible future scenarios bob and weave and sometimes collide with one another around the meeting table.

One council member, Teresa, grew up in the Southside Avenue neighborhood but now lives seven miles away. Her words reflect her concerns about the future: "The church down the street from my house is attracting members. Their new worship service features music with drums and guitars. My neighbor is a member. She says their minister attended a conference about new methods of outreach. Maybe we should send Andrea to a conference like that." Teresa wants Southside Avenue Church to be more appealing to her teenage sons. She also wants the church to give her sons tools for making good decisions as they journey the treacherous road to adulthood. "Contemporary worship does seem to work for some churches," replies Joe, a founding member of the church. "I'm just not sure that's what we need. I can remember a time when so many people came to worship here we needed a new sanctuary. That was long before anyone even heard of contemporary worship. Maybe we need to figure out what was making the church grow so much then. What do you think, Andrea?" Joe's question conveys his desire to validate the church's past.

Andrea considers Teresa's and Joe's observations. Teresa is right. Some church growth and renewal models have indeed become popular. But Andrea is reluctant to embrace any of them too quickly or wholeheartedly. Ministry models that sound innovative and life giving in a conference presentation or that are perfect for one congregation can seem an awkward fit or not be effective in another setting. Learning to translate new perspectives on ministry into the dialects of local congregations can be as difficult as translating Southside Avenue's enduring spirit of care and community into the multiple dialects of its changing neighborhood.

Though their observations reflect contrasting views, Tom and Teresa share a common concern. They, along with Andrea, realize that

Southside Avenue Church needs an infusion of energy and new life in its ministry. But Southside Avenue Church, like many other congregations, faces complex issues. For example, responding to the gospel call to go into Southside Avenue's surrounding neighborhood and make disciples will not by itself solve the congregation's financial problems. Making disciples will not automatically make ends meet.

One reason is that most of the immigrants within a half-mile radius of the church wrestle with financial troubles of their own, troubles resulting from language barriers, educational limits, and employment difficulties. Thus, even if Southside Avenue Church adopts the most up-to-date outreach models, a surge of local participation in the congregation may not overcome the current budget shortfall.

Andrea also realizes that reaching out to Latino and Latina neighbors is about more than finding solutions to congregational financial and attendance woes. The Latino and Latina community is rich with voices that hold unique and very personal sacred stories of lament and celebration. Southside Avenue Church can learn important theological lessons about community, mutual respect, and God *from and along with their Latino and Latina neighbors.* If their ministry is to be about more than making ends meet, Andrea and Southside Avenue need a plan that addresses their financial situation *and* equips them to embrace the call to be hospitable disciple makers.

Keep the Call grows out of the conviction that each congregation engenders unique stories of redemption and transformation whose wisdom cannot be found anyplace else. Healthy and life-giving approaches to ministry are rooted in these stories. Congregations gain clarity about their identities and nurture congregational health by exploring intersections between these stories and God's Story. At these intersections is the genesis of effective congregational ministries.

Keep the Call also encourages congregations and pastoral leaders to be more aware of the in-breaking of God's reign in neighborhoods like Southside—in the stories of people whose cultural roots are in other lands, in the hearts of people who have risked dangerous and difficult journeys across many kinds of borders, in the actions of people who hear God's call in different languages. These neighborhoods, like local congregations, engender unique wisdom about God, redemption, and faith.

If Andrea and Southside Avenue Church can revitalize their congregational story and identity *and* open their doors to theological insights available in their changing neighborhood, they may discover healthier and more holistic approaches to ministry.

An Invitation to a Process

Keep the Call is not an instruction manual. This is because life-giving approaches to ministry are not *products* and do not result in products. Giving birth to ministry is a creative *process* that requires the theological imaginations and commitments of the whole community and its leaders.

Enormous potential for congregational renewal and health awaits us in today's context. To tap into this potential, congregations and their leaders need processes that equip them to move through cultural ambiguities and communal difficulties in a spirit of creativity, faith, and hope. *Keep the Call* invites those who seek approaches to ministry that really work to bring their stories into conversation with these processes.

PART 1

Ministry as Proclamation

CHAPTER 1

Do   You   Hear
What   I   Hear?

*There are doubtless many different kinds of sounds in the world,
and nothing is without sound. (1 Corinthians 14:10)*

This chapter explores the soundscape of Christian congregational life: *ministry as proclamation*. God speaks. This is the genesis of Christian proclamation. Though communities do not always agree about what God's speaking sounds like, the recorded biblical witness of Jewish and Christian traditions tells the story of a God who calls and people of faith who respond.

God speaks in Genesis, and chaos becomes the womb for a cosmic creation animated by sound. God speaks in Exodus, and Miriam, tambourine in hand, leads the choral celebration of a liberated people. God speaks in John's Gospel, and a divine Word dances in the vestments of humanity. God speaks with fiery tongues in Acts, and Pentecostal flames enliven a communal voice unlike any heard before that time.

God still speaks today, and the sound of God's speaking is shaped into words by voices of people all over the world.[1] Even as God calls out to us, we call out to God. We also call out to one another and to the world. *Ministry as proclamation* is all of these things: hearing God's voice (vocation), discerning one's own voice (ministerial formation), and learning to use our voices to proclaim the gospel within the community and to the world (prophetic witness).

In *The Tuning of the World*, environmentalist and musician R. Murray Schafer uses an intriguing term—"soundscape"—to talk about the world's sounds. According to Schafer, a soundscape is all of the sounds that make up a particular acoustical field or location.[2] Sounds of God's call and human response have been historically and still are significant frequencies on the world's soundscape.

This chapter invites readers to pay attention to local and global soundscapes, alert to the peculiar sounds of what we call Christian proclamation. A question shapes the chapter's discussion: How can congregations effectively communicate God's good news to the world?

Some Theological Foundations for Our Listening Experiment

Ministry as proclamation is found where God's voice and human voices come together. Writing about preaching, Mary Donovan Turner and Mary Lin Hudson speak insightfully about this human-divine intersection: "The Holy Spirit, sacred *ruach*, breathes through women and men, old and young, single and married, slaves and free persons, Jew and non-Jew, and empowers them to speak with authority and truth.... To be made in the image of God is to be made in the sound of God."[3]

"Made in the sound of God." When Anna Julia Cooper first spoke this phrase in the late 1800s, it was both unfamiliar and unexpected. As a black woman fighting to be heard in a world resistant to her voice, Cooper insisted that all people are created not only in the image of God but also in the sound of God. All people, her voice heralded, are called by God. All people have the right to proclaim the gospel. All people also have a responsibility to give voice to God's promises of justice and hope.[4]

Cooper's words dance across the pages of history to stir pastoral leaders and congregations today. Each of us is called to embody ministry *as proclamation*. Committed to this call, many pastoral leaders rummage books, and search the Internet and other resources for the "right" model for proclaiming the gospel effectively. Two questions invite a different approach:

- What if leaders and congregations stop chasing the myth of the "perfect" model for ministry and instead energize their own identities and voices as resources for gospel proclamation?
- What if Christian proclamation is energized not only by God's transcendent voice but also by God's indwelling voice?

3

Kristin Linklater's approach to voice training provides an analogy for setting free the indwelling voice of God. Linklater's goal as a voice instructor is "to liberate the natural voice rather than to develop a vocal technique."[5] Theologian Stephen Webb shares some of Linklater's convictions. "The voice," Webb asserts, "is not superimposed on the body."[6] Rather, voice, soul, and body are interconnected.

Linklater argues that a speaker's "natural voice" comes through when defenses acquired along life's journey cease to limit expression. These defenses emerge as a result of life experiences such as discrimination or public ridicule.

Linklater describes the natural voice that emerges when these defenses break down: "Such a voice is a built-in attribute of the body with an innate potential for a wide pitch range, intricate harmonics and kaleidoscopic textural qualities. . . . The natural voice is transparent—revealing, not describing, inner impulses of emotion and thought. . . . The *person* is heard, not the person's voice. To free the voice is to free the person."[7] How do Linklater's words about the natural voice relate to ministry as proclamation? Freeing authentic voices and thus persons is vital to cultivating Spirit-infused ministry as proclamation. This is because gospel proclamation resonates from within people who have both freedom and authenticity to speak truth as they understand it.

Freeing voices and persons is also connected to theological reflection, an action of faith vital to ministry as proclamation. What is theological reflection? Our definition begins with Scripture. In Genesis, God creates by speaking. This divine duet of creation and vocalization motivates human contemplation of God. It also motivates self-contemplation and contemplation of human relationships.

This contemplative work is sometimes called theological reflection. Theological reflection invites people to listen more carefully to their daily lives for God's creation-vocalization duet. In other words, theological reflection is one way for congregations and pastoral leaders to become more aware of intersections between their voices and God's voice.

Several questions serve as key signatures for theological listening and reflection:

- Do our proclamations reflect the tones and timbres of God's voice?
- Do our voices passionately communicate the gospel's claims of justice, freedom, and peace?

4

- Do our proclamations take up the real struggles of people in our congregations, neighborhood, and world?
- What steps do we need to take to hear echoes of God's voice in voices unlike ours?

Hearing God's Voice

The voice of the LORD is over the waters;
    the God of glory thunders,
    the LORD, over mighty waters.
The voice of the LORD is powerful;
    the voice of the LORD is full of majesty.

        . . .

The voice of the LORD causes the oaks to whirl,
    and strips the forest bare;
    and in his temple all say, "Glory!" (Psalm 29:3-4, 9)

"Can you help me hear God's voice?" The question met Andrea at the church door following a sermon based on Psalm 29. The question and the voice that spoke it haunt her.

Helping people hear God's voice is a complex pastoral venture. The sounds of Southside Avenue's neighborhood fluctuate daily as a growing number of immigrants rent houses in the area. Andrea speaks little Spanish. Many of Southside Avenue Church's new neighbors speak little English. Hearing God's voice in the Southside community is as basic and as difficult as translating between two different cultures and languages.

Efforts to hear God's voice mark the everyday lives of people in Andrea's congregation in other ways as well. For example, several members face decisions about nursing home care for aging parents. One father worries about the safety of a child summoned to military service in Iraq. These congregants strain their ears for a word from God.

In fact, the question at the church door that Sunday was less about theological doctrine or the church's public voice than about how the woman asking the question could make it through another week: *"I try to pray but can't concentrate. God doesn't answer. Or maybe I can't hear God. Can you help me hear God's voice?"*

The church member's question is timely and multilayered. Changes in Southside Avenue's soundscape affect physical hearing and listening.

Changes in the soundscape also affect theological hearing and listening. Stepping out of the church doors late Monday afternoon, Andrea experiences the acoustical deluge of rush-hour traffic on a street that several decades ago echoed with the rumble of only a handful of cars an hour. She walks down the street. Lively conversation in front of a convenience store falters as a Mexican clerk shifts linguistic gears from Spanish to a halting English "hello."

Distant church bells sound the hour. The dulcet tones hearken back to a time when church bells were sacred acoustic calendars. In those days, the bells' tones rose authoritatively above everyday noises to announce births, deaths, marriages, and other significant community happenings.[8] The carillon Andrea hears on this Monday ring from a local university chapel. They sound the five o'clock hour each weekday and sometimes mark special events such as graduations. These chapel bells still attract the community's attention, but their twenty-first-century tones seem more ornamental than authoritative.

Hearing the bells as a reflective starting point, Andrea wonders how or if congregations like Southside Avenue can again speak with authority along these streets. How are Christian people to herald God's tidings in a world noisy with competing proclamations? Can Southside Avenue congregation's ministry nurture symphonic moments when God's voice cuts through the chaos with sounds of peace and redemption? Can a predominantly Anglo congregation proclaim God's grace effectively within a predominantly Latino and Latina neighborhood? Can Southside Avenue Church help people hear God's voice?

Discovering New Gospel Soundboards

Andrea believes the answer to the above questions is "yes." But on some days her "yes" is punctuated by a hesitant question mark rather than a resounding exclamation point. Some of Andrea's uncertainty has to do with how she understands proclamation.

Andrea is a child of robust Protestant preaching traditions. Her grandfather was a Baptist preacher. Andrea learned at her grandfather's knee and later in seminary classrooms that preaching is powerful speech. Preaching changes lives. Preaching changes worlds. For Andrea and other Protestant pastoral leaders and congregations, biblical preaching—

proclaiming God's Word from a pulpit during worship—is the heart and soul of ministry as proclamation.

Recently, Andrea was introduced to a new term that is redefining her understanding of proclamation. She heard a piano technician speak one night about a piano's *soundboard*. A grand piano's soundboard is constructed of thin pieces of wood fit together into a solid sheet. Strings are anchored on one end by tuning pins, stretched across the soundboard, and anchored on the other end to a hitch pin. Wooden *bridges* attached to the soundboard suspend and hold the tension of the strings. When struck by the piano's hammers, the strings vibrate: "The sound of piano strings vibrating is rather feeble, so the volume is increased by use of a **soundboard**, a large, thin wooden diaphragm.... Wooden **bridges**, against which the strings press, transfer the strings' vibrations to the soundboard. The soundboard increases the volume of sound because it moves more air than the strings could alone."[9] To state this another way, the soundboard amplifies the sounds of the vibrating strings.

Put more concretely, when the pianist at Southside Avenue Church plays, her fingers dancing across the keys in the hymnic patterns of "How Great Thou Art" or "I Love to Tell the Story," the soundboard does its work. It amplifies the strings' vibrations and congregants are able to hear the notes and chords.

Andrea was surprised to learn that some churches have *architectural* soundboards. Before the invention of electronic amplification, architects designed some pulpits with soundboards. The purpose of the soundboards was to amplify preachers' voices. The pulpit of a local Episcopal church has a soundboard. To Andrea, the soundboard in that church resembles a wooden lid. The soundboard is suspended about four feet above the pulpit. Historically, when a preacher gave voice to God's Word, this soundboard amplified the proclamation so it could be heard by more people from greater distances.

Andrea has begun to realize that Gospel soundboards exist in places other than church buildings. In fact, soundboards for God's Word can be found anywhere that people created in the sound of God talk and listen to one another—restaurants, classrooms, board rooms, or street corners.

That this is the case is a testimony to how God's Spirit transforms the vibrations of diverse voices into proclamations of gospel news. Everyday talk, enlivened by God's Spirit, becomes sacred conversation, rich with amplifications of God's grace.[10] People created in the sound of God help one another hear God's voice.

Gospel Proclamation as a Community "Soundmark"

Even a generic definition illustrates the distinct role of proclamation in the larger arena of communication. According to one dictionary, a proclamation is "an official formal public announcement (as a public notice, edict, decree)."[11] Proclamation carries voiceprints of confidence and force. Listen to the energetic authority in this catalog of synonyms. To proclaim is to "announce, declare, profess, herald, publish, broadcast, make known, signal, knell, cry, blare, trumpet, reveal, decree, rule, pronounce."[12]

What Andrea has begun to realize is that these spirited words depict Southside Avenue Church's past more than they animate its present. The same is true for other congregations. The university carillon comes to mind again in relation to this. The retreat of church bells to ornamental acoustic margins symbolizes something larger about the role of congregations and proclamation in people's lives today.

Webb relates the shift in the authority of congregational proclamation to contemporary perceptions of God's voice. Many people today, he writes, treat spirituality primarily as "an inner awareness of the divine."[13] Webb's point is well taken. Inner spiritual awareness has become an increasingly popular focus of religious life.

Inner spiritual awareness is indeed vital to healthy faith. But proclamation leads to more than spiritual self-awareness. Proclamation *trumpets*. Proclamation *heralds*. And gospel proclamation? The gospel is radical news of freedom and grace. Gospel proclaimers are called to embrace this news internally. We are also called to trumpet and herald it with a public force that liberates and empowers.

What has happened in Southside Avenue Church is that members have become less confident about both inner spiritual awareness and public faith expression. One reason is the changing sonic environment. Schafer uses another term, "soundmarks," to refer to distinct or specially regarded communal sounds.[14] In the Southside Avenue neighborhood, soundmarks are changing.

Some Southside Avenue members are startled by contrasts between soundmarks that molded their childhoods and soundmarks that today greet their grandchildren's ears. Joe's experience is an example. Now a Southside Avenue Church council member, Joe grew up in the Southside neighborhood to the sounds of tractors churning the fields and owls calling to the moon.

Some soundmarks from Joe's childhood endure. Backyard owls still hoot at the moon. But now the owl's nightly proclamations battle sonic competition from sirens or from the rumble of eighteen-wheelers on the nearby interstate. Also, in that patch of ground where tractor engines once provided familiar sounds? The new tenant in that field is now a big-box retailer instead of a farmer's herd of beef cattle. Parking lot sounds have replaced farming sounds.

Joe and others in the church sometimes struggle to distinguish God's voice from other noises in this changing sonic environment. Or, as Andrea prefers to think of it, they struggle to hear God's voice in new tones and timbres. In fact, though no one on the council addresses it directly, nostalgia for "the way things used to be," along with worries about the future, mask a deeper theological concern: Does God sound the same as when our church was thriving? We could hear God more clearly then, and the neighborhood seemed to pay more attention to our voice. If God's voice sounds different now, how will we recognize God's voice?

One thing the Southside Avenue congregation must resist is too much nostalgia for past soundmarks. A realistic connection with the past is important. But in order to be effective gospel proclaimers today, Southside Avenue and other congregations need to avoid putting past successes *or* failures at the center of current ministries.

The reason? All history is ambiguous, including the history of Christianity and Christian congregations. Christianity has been and continues to be a voice of hope in a troubled world. However, some Christians, past and present, have also supported slavery or been silent in the face of violence.

Likewise, histories of individual congregations are mixed. At times, congregations have boldly heralded gospel truths in the face of injustices in their neighborhoods and the world. Congregations have at other times been less prophetic, colluding with voices that do not support freedom or peace.

This brings our discussion back to an emphasis on theological reflection. Congregations and pastoral leaders are always *in the process* of learning how to foster Spirit-infused proclamation. They are thus called to make a commitment *to the process*. Theological reflection is central to the process.

Congregations and pastoral leaders committed to theological reflection become more open to the blessings *and* blights of their past. They become alert to unhealthy voices embedded in their histories. They also learn to use their voices to challenge those things in their communities and even those things in their own stories that perpetuate injustice.[15]

Southside Avenue Church's decision to call Andrea as pastor exemplifies the value of theological reflection about the past. Andrea will never forget her first pastoral conversation with Marie, a seventy-five-year-old church member. "Finally!" Marie exclaimed. "I never thought I would see it in my lifetime, but it's actually happened. When I was your age, I wanted to preach. I told my pastor. He said I would make a great Sunday school teacher. I don't think he even heard what I was saying. But you are here now and people are listening to you."

Andrea is Southside Avenue Church's first female pastor. Her voice in the pulpit has brought to Southside Avenue a new soundmark. This new soundmark is unfamiliar and perhaps even uncomfortable to some people in the congregation. Many of them never imagined hearing God's voice in the vocal frequencies of a woman speaking from their pulpit.

Yet, Southside Avenue's pastoral call to Andrea points to the congregation's ability to imagine its voice in ways that depart from history and tradition. Now, Andrea and Southside Avenue Church must tap into this ability in order to imagine other parts of their story in new ways. When they do this reflective and imaginative work, they are doing theological reflection.

Proclamation and Today's Acoustical Palette

One of the gifts of today's acoustical palette is its ability to hold old sounds in novel ways while adding new sounds. However, as Schafer and Webb point out, the expansion of sounds is a mixed blessing. As sounds multiply, a perplexing theological puzzle emerges: Can our pipe organs and hymns, our voices raised in prayer—all those sacred sounds that are a cherished part of Christian tradition—still get the community's attention? In the midst of today's noise, how will we know that the voice we hear and call sacred is God's? Can a predominantly Anglo congregation proclaim God's grace effectively to a predominantly Latino and Latina neighborhood?

The world's acoustical palette began to expand with the advent of industrialization. Industrialization accented the orchestra of everyday sounds with the whirs and clangs of new machinery—steam engines, power looms, and threshing machines, just to name a few. Over time, these sounds became more familiar. Industries grew. Factory owners began to keep machines buzzing and humming day and night with around-the-clock work hours. City populations—and noises—mushroomed.

Many of the hums and buzzes of industrialization endure today. They are joined by new sounds ranging from cell phones, to supersonic jets, to leisure time sound makers such as snowmobiles, speedboats, and MP3 players. A number of the sources of these new sounds improve people's lives. For example, coast-to-coast distances between loved ones' voices shrink with the push of a telephone button, amplification makes it possible to hear more voices more clearly, and sounds of distant lands and dialects reverberate from radios or televisions, making listeners aware of the wonders and difficulties of life in other places.

On some days these technological advances mean we are less quick to make uneducated or unfair judgments about people whose lives are different from ours. But on other days sounds are so accessible that even the groans of human suffering become little more than ambient noise as we move through our daily activities. In other words, the Information Age creates an environment where we hear a greater diversity of sounds but where listening is much trickier.

On many days, Webb writes, we are bombarded by more aural information than we can hear or process with any real clarity.[16] This contemporary reality is not without consequences. The noisier our lives are, the more difficult it is to hear—the creaks and coos of the wind and woods, the music of the spheres, the comforting or cautioning cadences of one another's voices. So, too, the noisier our lives are, the more difficult it is to be heard.

One consequence of the recent swell of sounds is described by John L. Locke in *The De-Voicing of Society*. "Info-speech," he writes, is gradually replacing face-to-face conversation: "Now, the exchange of information is too often the reason for speech, the personal relationship relegated to a position of secondary importance.... Our great-grandparents ... could see and hear their communicants. Messages were wrapped in blankets of feeling. Voices moved. Faces flashed.... We great-grandchildren trade thoughts on a daily basis with people we do not know and will never meet."[17] Locke's assessment reflects more than nostalgia for a less sound-saturated past. The contemporary appetite for information shapes most communication today, and the impersonal efficiency of "info-speech" daily leaves its imprint on human relationships.

Examples of information infatuation abound. A new media vocabulary seasons daily speech—talking heads, sound bites, spin doctors. Around-the-clock newscasts on cable television networks, local television networks, and satellite radio bombard our ears. Simultaneous to spoken news reports, written messages crawl along the bottom of television screens to flood our eyes, moving with almost dizzying speed from disaster headlines to college basketball scores. Also, the expanding stickiness of the World Wide Web draws new cybernauts to its charms and dangers every day.[18]

Many people scramble to find a quiet center in the swirl of the information hurricane. Recognizing the onslaught, some churches offer themselves as that stabilizing center. They promise safety and rest for those buffeted by life's noise and activity. But whether or not churches promise sanctuary, none are immune to complex issues raised by the information hurricane itself.

Homiletician Brad Braxton thus extends a clarion call to churches and pastoral leaders: "Not enough people are asking this question: Does *more* information necessarily mean *better* information?" Braxton insists that the role of the preacher is to "provide God's news that people can use."[19] What is this news we can use? How do gospel proclaimers and listeners ferret out God's news from the sound-bite barrage? What can churches realistically offer to people wearied by life's chaos and uncertainty?

Even associated theological questions, though important, can seem overwhelming: Who should we endorse as legitimate proclaimers of God's news? Whose voices should we resist or ignore? Do we have a responsibility to tone down or silence destructive or oppressive voices? Before simply cranking up the decibels so that congregational proclamations can be heard over the din of contemporary noise, careful consideration of questions like these is vital. We can begin such a consideration by exploring the "acoustical dimensions" of the principal source of Christian proclamation: God's Word.

The Acoustical Design of God's Word

Andrea sometimes marvels at the seeming outlandishness of Christian proclamation. On 52 of 365 days of the year, she and other preachers continue a tradition rejected by many teachers, newscasters, and other public personalities in today's media-blitzed era. Preachers stand behind a podium and proclaim a message based on an ancient sacred text, the Bible. *And people gather to listen*.

What is the lure of this weekly act of proclamation? One answer may be embedded in that question at the church door: "Can you help me hear God's voice?" Braxton makes a valid point. What many Sunday-morning listeners want is "news they can use." What many Sunday morning listeners want is to hear God speaking *to them*.

This places enormous responsibility on the preacher. But ministry as proclamation is about more than what is proclaimed from the pulpit. As discussed earlier, ministry as proclamation has to do with setting free all people's voices to speak God's Word in their daily words and actions. More needs to be said at this point about connections between the work of setting voices free and the oral dimensions of God's Word.

Before the Christian tradition became primarily a "religion of the book," historian William Graham writes, proclaiming the "good news" orally "took precedence over any scriptural authority accorded to Jewish holy writ or early Christian writings.... Put simply, the word of God was the gospel message of the risen Christ long before it was a book or collection of books."[20] God's Word was and is, first and foremost, a spoken word or a proclaimed word. Webb echoes this. The Bible "was written for the ear more than the eye," he asserts. "The Word of God is never more at home, so to speak, than in the sound of the human voice."[21]

Who, then, is charged with speaking God's Word? Preachers, certainly, but others, too, bear the responsibility and are given the gift of proclamation. What we know of life in the early church testifies to multifaceted oral traditions of gospel proclamation. Before stories about Jesus' life and teachings were written down, they were remembered aloud. Community leaders shared stories of Jesus through preaching and teaching. But other believers also became proclaimers as they remembered and recounted, often around meal tables, how Jesus' life had affected them.

Reinvigorating the oral dimensions of gospel news requires that pastoral leaders and congregations embody the polyphonic nature of the Bible's written words. God speaks through and in many voices in Scripture. The four-voiced testimony of the Gospels of Matthew, Mark, Luke, and John exemplifies this. The same is true today. God speaks in and to our age when biblical truth is voiced anew in the diverse voices of people in local congregations and neighborhoods, both as they worship together and as they go about their daily lives.[22] In other words, because people are created in the sound of God, their voices are sacred.

When we acknowledge human voices as sacred, countless possibilities for gospel proclamation emerge. Weekly acts of reading Scripture in worship provide examples. Consider depths of meaning made possible when a teenage girl reads Matthew's version of the "sermon on the plain" and an unlikely duet of her voice with Jesus' voice is created. Or imagine what gospel truths are heralded when a grandmother reads Luke's Magnificat, her aging voice merging with Mary's youthful singing. Or explore the theological questions generated when a new father reads from the Psalms and, along with that ancient hymn writer, probes life's uncertainties.

Ample material for theological reflection also emerges in moments like these. What did Jesus' voice sound like? What does God sound like today? Who among us are unlikely gospel proclaimers? These questions point to a valuable insight about ministry as proclamation. In worship, the Bible's written words become a living sacred soundscape—God's Word—as Scripture is spoken aloud by people who wrestle everyday with both possibilities and limits of their humanity.

Pastoral leaders have the responsibility of facilitating deeper contemplation of echoes of God's voice in human voices. This process of theological reflection can happen through worship, in educational programs, or even during pastoral visits. Often, people are not aware of the beauty and power of their voices and words. Over time, as congregants become better equipped to hear God's voice in their own and others' voices, they become more energized to proclaim God's Word. They also become better equipped to infuse everyday talk with language that cultivates God's grace.

The Bible depicts the power of God's spoken Word when, in Luke's Gospel, Jesus reads aloud the words of the prophet Isaiah:

> When he came to Nazareth, where he had been brought up, he went to the synagogue on the sabbath day, as was his custom. He stood up to read, and the scroll of the prophet Isaiah was given to him. He unrolled the scroll and found the place where it was written:

> "The Spirit of the Lord is upon me,
>   because he has anointed me to bring good news to the poor.
> He has sent me to proclaim release to the captives
>   and recovery of sight to the blind,
>   to let the oppressed go free,
>   to proclaim the year of the Lord's favor."

And he rolled up the scroll, gave it back to the attendant, and sat down. The eyes of all in the synagogue were fixed on him. Then he began to say to them, "Today this scripture has been fulfilled in your hearing." (Luke 4:16-21)

Read aloud by Jesus in synagogue worship, words and phrases recorded in the sacred scroll of Isaiah become new again. Ancient promises dance to life. Spoken in worship in a time and place different from their original writing, Isaiah's promises disrupt business as usual with a proclamation of what is radically *not* business as usual: "release to the captives," "recovering of sight to the blind," liberty to those who are oppressed.

What makes acts of public reading disruptive? Public speaking becomes gospel proclamation, theologian Rebecca Chopp says, "through anointing . . . for no matter how careful one's preparation, or loud one's voice, or artistic one's strategy, there remains the claim of anointing in the Spirit."[23] In this text from Luke, Jesus embraces his "anointed" identity as a preacher. The Spirit has anointed *him* to preach good news. He heralds Isaiah's ancient prophecies and declares them fulfilled even as listeners hear them *in that time and place.* Proclaiming such news to people trapped in oppressive and limiting structures in any era is without a doubt disruptive as well as liberating activity.

These reflections hold empowering wisdom for busy preachers who face the pressing weekly reality that Sunday is coming. Setting free human voices to proclaim good news is not work pastoral leaders do alone. Pastoral leaders *and* congregants do this sacred work in community, buoyed up by one another and by the anointing of the Spirit.

What do these reflections have to do with congregations like Southside Avenue's? All congregations, even those facing difficult times, can be and are anointed by God's Spirit to proclaim gospel news. The promise and hope of this anointing are profound. God's Word is birthed in our humanity—our spirits, minds, and voices. Thus, God's Word is birthed in worshiping congregations who embody God's Spirit. Perhaps even more profound and potentially disruptive of oppressive structures, God's Word is birthed not only when we preach but also when we use everyday words and actions to resist anything that destroys spirits or bodies created in the sound of God.

Acts of proclamation take different forms depending on congregational characteristics such as size, location, and theological perspective. But when any congregation says "yes" to the call to proclaim in everyday speech and actions God's promises of healing and release, that proclamation almost certainly heralds news that attracts listeners. It just as certainly slams into an assortment of forces resistant to change. Yet, to speak the gospel's words of freedom, perhaps especially in the face of resistant forces, is to proclaim news that emboldens people to set free their voices and in doing so to set free their bodies and souls.

Creating Sacred Conversations

Recently, Andrea has begun to explore a new idea: What if ministry as proclamation begins with the communion table rather than the pulpit? Andrea believes more passionately each day that Anna Julia Cooper was right. All of God's people are called to proclaim the gospel. Thus, she is committed to working with church members to seek anew, *as a community*, their own "true speech" about God and faith.[24] The communion table may be a good starting place for this work.

One example of the sacred speech shaped at the communion table is related to the presence of the table itself. Tables are powerful symbols. Tables represent being served and serving. Tables are places of conversations, laughter, arguments, and reconciliations.[25]

Tables also symbolize generosity and hospitality. At tables, we learn how to share with one another, and we learn what it is like when people do not share. When tables are places of hospitality, the people who gather around them learn skills for transforming other life tables into generous and hospitable tables. At hospitable tables, people are also empowered to risk open and honest conversation. Space is created where sacred conversation can become world-changing proclamation. We consider now what this might entail at Southside Avenue Church.

One end of Marlon's kitchen table has become a storage space for tools—a hammer, several sizes of screwdrivers, and other nuts and bolts of his life as a carpenter. Coffee cups and pill bottles clutter the other end of the table. A photo of his deceased wife magnetically clings to the refrigerator overlooking it all.

Marlon's table holds many stories. When he comes to the Lord's Table at Southside Avenue Church, Marlon brings his kitchen table stories with him. What do Jesus' biblical words of remembrance at that ancient Last Supper table have to do with Marlon's kitchen table?

Linda also brings her kitchen table stories to the Lord's Table. In fact, a question from her kitchen table found its way into Andrea's ears: "Can you help me hear God's voice?" Linda sits nightly at her kitchen table, juggling too little income and too many bills. She regularly does this while she and her children eat dinner. In Mark's Gospel, Jesus multiplies loaves and fishes and feeds a crowd of hungry listeners. What do Jesus' actions at that ancient outdoor "table" have to do with Linda's kitchen table?

A similar question can be posed in relation to Sandra's supper table. Painful stories season Sandra's participation at Southside Avenue's communion table. Though no one in the church knows it, Sandra's husband often erupts in violence at the supper table. During communion at Southside Avenue Church, Andrea breaks bread and speaks ancient words taken from 1 Corinthians: "The body of Christ broken for you." What do these words have to do with Sandra's table story?

Learning skills for appropriate sharing of stories like these around the communion table is a key to collaborative ministries of proclamation. So, too, is learning how to do theological reflection about these stories. Andrea knows this is not easy. People's life stories are messy, and are not always comfortable to tell or listen to.

Yet, skill in sacred conversation and theological reflection is essential. Congregations cannot take up the real struggles of people in their neighborhoods and world without it. They cannot authentically proclaim God's news of freedom and grace until they learn to hear God's voice in the experiences of others.

Homiletician Lucy Atkinson Rose uses another table symbol to underscore these communal aspects of Christian proclamation: "roundtable" preaching. Speaking in tandem with Anna Julia Cooper, Rose insists that all people are called to preach. All people are called to voice their stories in light of God's Story.[26]

For Southside Avenue Church, this means something more than inviting Marlon, Linda, and Sandra to the Lord's Table. It also means learning to listen to them *as gospel proclaimers*. This is vital to setting free natural voices of faith. People are called to listen and speak such that they set one another free to proclaim God's truth, even when that truth is painful to speak or hear.

What is the role of pastoral leaders in this process? Homiletician John McClure encourages pastoral leaders to interact *"with"* hearers before speaking *"for and to"* them from the pulpit.[27] For this to happen effectively, pastoral leaders have to balance two responsibilities. They must listen theologically and pastorally to congregations, biblical traditions, and broader cultural soundscape. At the same time, they must seek the authenticity of their own voices. Healthy leadership of ministry as proclamation is born at the intersection of these two pastoral responsibilities.

Equally vital to sacred conversation is learning to welcome new conversation partners. McClure emphasizes that we hear God's voice when we look in our neighbors' faces and "experience an absolute obligation toward compassion, resistance, justice, and hope that grips our lives and holds us to a new vision for all humanity."[28] As discussed earlier, many of Southside Avenue Church's neighbors speak a language unfamiliar to church members. They sing different hymns. Their tables hold different sacred stories.

Listening into and through these differences is an important skill. Such listening expands a congregation's dictionary of sacred soundmarks to include hymns and stories of neighbors who are not church members. Thus, such listening cultivates hospitality and spiritual growth. But this kind of listening also involves risk. When we really listen to one another, we make ourselves vulnerable to voices that could radically change how we hear God's voice. Even so, saying "yes" to God's call to nurture sacred conversation is essential if congregations and pastoral leaders desire more authentic, Spirit-infused ministries.

A Sound Theology of Ministry

Faith requires both speaking and listening. Proclamation involves both speaking and listening. Gordon Lathrop speaks of the "astonishing" character of what we proclaim in our Sunday worship: "Neither public nor intimate, this speech tells the truth simply; it addresses God and other invisible realities directly; it unhesitatingly uses metaphors and images; it does not shrink from naming death and failure nor from unfeignedly expressing joy; it calls people, without ceremony, by their first names; it works economically, frequently falling back into a silence."[29]

But proclamation does not end with Sunday worship's benediction. Congregations are called to contribute unique theological and spiritual frequencies to everyday soundscapes.

This call to hear and give voice to God's Word everyday makes communal and public demands of pastoral leaders and congregations. In other words, God's Word provokes. God's Word in Exodus provokes with stirring proclamations of freedom. God promises exodus from oppression today. How do we proclaim this promise realistically in a world where so many people long to be set free?

God's Word in Revelation also provokes. In Revelation, John eats God's scroll and finds it "sweet as honey" in his mouth but bitter to his stomach. How do we take up the bittersweet work of making God's promises digestible today?

Scripture's provocative words call congregations and pastoral leaders to herald radical gospel news. Sometimes our proclamations resound with clarity. They trumpet joyously. At other times, however, our proclamations lack finesse. They are clumsy and uncertain. But the rather astonishing fact remains. As we make our way out onto today's highways, church bells of a sort continue to beckon, at least symbolically, in our voices. Even in congregations unsure of how to speak boldly amid the clamor of competing sounds, the call and commitment to proclamation can endure.

The hope of the future strangely rests in this endurance as it both enlivens thriving congregations and sustains struggling congregations. But a caveat is in order. As suggested earlier, another kind of commitment also cradles future hope: a commitment to theological reflection. This is a commitment all congregations can nurture because theological reflection is a skill congregations can learn.

Resolute trumpeting is no substitute for depths of proclamation made possible when congregations are committed to honest conversation and theological reflection. Congregations and pastoral leaders who risk this commitment entertain a process of spiritual growth that celebrates mysterious dimensions of God's Word. This means that they temper what they are certain they know with a humble recognition of how much they do not know. Ironically, perhaps even miraculously, somewhere in this tension, genuine proclamation is birthed—in actions, words, convictions, and values.

The next chapter explores some approaches to building these kinds of proclamation skills.

CHAPTER 2

Sound Approaches to Ministry as Proclamation

Two months ago Grace Community Church opened the doors to a new "sanctuary in the round." Leaders designed Grace Church's ministries specifically to attract Generation Xers. No pipe organs or traditional hymns echo in Grace Church. Instead, the electronic vibrations of synthesizers and electric guitars ripple through the sanctuary during the Sunday worship hours.

Yes, worship *hours*. Eighteen months after its inaugural worship service, Grace Church's attendance outgrew a temporary storefront gathering space. Now, the gospel is proclaimed *twice* each Sunday in the new sanctuary, and another service is on the drawing board.

Grace Church's upbeat energy is alluring. Andrea sometimes looks with longing at the new building and packed parking lot. Adding new members is a financial necessity for Southside Avenue Church, and more important, Andrea and other Southside Avenue members genuinely want people to hear the gospel. They want people to encounter God *at Southside Avenue Church*.

Grace Community Church represents a number of lively voices on the North American congregational soundscape. Some of these congregations' ministerial models are respected and emulated across the United States. An example is the "purpose-driven church" model, made popular by pastoral leader Rick Warren.

The phenomenal growth of Warren's congregation in California is alluring. Pastoral leaders of congregations large and small study Warren's ministry books and attend his leadership workshops. A persistent question fuels these leaders' interest in Warren's purpose-driven church: "How can I transport some of the energy and success of the purpose-driven model to my own congregation?"

Some concepts in models like Warren's are helpful regardless of congregational size, denominational affiliation, or location. Warren's main spiritual rallying cry, for example, heralds that all people are created by God for a purpose. This confidently proclaimed theological conviction has infused countless despairing souls and struggling congregations with hope and new direction.

But a caution is in order. Ministry models that work for some churches may not be realistic or healthy for other congregations. Warren's foundational concepts are important. People are indeed created by God. God calls all people, and all people have vocations. But along with these concepts, congregations need to consider another, often overlooked, insight about congregational health and growth.

Congregations have rich resources for proclamation embedded in their own identities and spiritual imaginations. Congregations and pastoral leaders sometimes work too hard to be like Grace Community Church or other "successful" churches. As a result, they overlook or even devalue these resources.

Put another way, every congregation is a treasure trove of wisdom about God. When a congregation lives out its distinct identity in its particular time and place, this wisdom comes to life. What keeps congregations from cultivating their unique theological wisdom? Multiple obstacles stand in the way. Some congregations have lost sight of who they are. Or they are too tired from conflict or other organizational struggles to imagine a different kind of future.

This chapter describes ways to nurture gospel proclamation rooted in distinct congregational identities. Three areas are the focus:

1. Theological *soundwalking*;
2. Competent and generous listening;
3. Dynamic gospel proclaiming.

Theological Soundwalking

Healthy, life-giving ministry does not come from the application of a template. In fact, one-size-fits-all patterns for ministry do not exist. To echo an insight from chapter 1, "the voice is not superimposed on the body." Life-giving ministry emerges when congregations and leaders learn to listen for God's voice and call *within* their own and their community's voices and identities.

This means, for example, that Andrea and Southside Avenue Church need to listen with fresh ears to their congregational voice. They also need to learn how to listen more attentively for God's voice in their changing community. Soundwalking is one way for congregations and their leaders to become more theologically sensitive to their acoustic surroundings.

Soundwalk Guidelines

The term *soundwalk* can be traced to the World Soundscape Project. Environmentalist R. Murray Schafer and a group of musicians and ecologists started the World Soundscape Project in the late 1960s to raise environmental acoustic awareness. Advocates of the Project coined the term *soundwalk* and developed soundwalk purposes and guidelines.

A soundwalk is an organized walk designed to help people focus more attentively on the sounds they hear in neighborhoods, agricultural areas, or other environments.[1] Soundwalks can be free-form but are usually guided by written or verbal instruction.

Soundwalk instructions are sometimes called "scores," bringing to mind the musicality of sound. Sounds heard on several soundwalks developed by the World Soundscape Project, for example, have been recorded and are considered musical compositions. Such a perspective on sounds suggests that multiple everyday acoustical environments—cafes, grocery stores, parks, restaurants, hospitals—can be thought of as musical environments. Soundwalking encourages walkers to listen to sounds from this perspective.

The following is a sample "soundwalk score." The score is adapted from a poetic text written by acoustic ecologist Hildegard Westerkamp.[2]

A Sample Soundwalk Score

Preparing for a Soundwalk
- Turn off the sounds in your head that create too much noise for you to hear the environment around you.
- Prepare your ears and mind for listening. For example, some soundwalkers preface their walks with a period of silence.

Some Questions to Guide a Soundwal
- What are the loudest sounds you hear?
- What are the quietest sounds?
- Which sounds have the lowest pitch? The highest pitch?
- Which sounds are most familiar? Least familiar?
- What rhythms do you hear?
- Do any sounds intrude as particularly loud, startling, or sharp?
- Do any sounds seem out of place for this environment?
- What do your footsteps sound like in the midst of these sounds?
- Can you hear the sound of your own voice? How loud would you have to talk to be heard?

A soundwalk score can guide a walk in its entirety. In that case, the walk's leader uses questions like those above to create an acoustical map of the environment. Or a version of the above score can be repeated at different stages of the walk.

For example, walkers may want to stop at points where they hear a significant acoustical change in the environment or where a particular sound grabs their attention. These are points where a score can guide more focused listening and exploration. Walkers may also want to take notes or make audio recordings of the walk.

Crucial to all soundwalks is attentive *listening*. Walkers may want to stop and reflect theologically at particular points along the walk, perhaps at those places where communal soundmarks are most clearly heard—or noticeably no longer heard. Or reflection can happen at the end of a walk. During moments of actual soundwalking, however, the most important task of the walker is to listen.

Soundwalking and Theological Reflection

Soundwalks are designed to increase awareness of acoustic environments. They are also designed to make walkers more aware of their acoustical impact on environments. *Theological* soundwalking shares these goals and has some specific aims of its own:

- to make persons of faith more aware of the spiritual dimensions of environmental sounds;
- to encourage persons of faith to listen to their environments as musical compositions that contain melodies of faith;
- to help congregations be more aware of how their communal sounds (preaching, worship, prayer, outreach, etc.) function as a spiritual acoustic presence in their neighborhoods;
- to give congregations and pastoral leaders disciplined practices for listening with open ears and hearts for the sounds of God in their neighborhoods.

With these theological aims in mind, congregations may want to participate in a four-part soundwalk exercise:

1. The soundwalk
2. Theological reflection on the soundwalk
3. A time to map and remember historical soundmarks
4. A time to listen into the future

Theological Reflection on a Soundwalk

The first part of a congregational soundwalk exercise is the soundwalk itself, guided by a soundwalk score like the one above. Concluding a soundwalk with guided discussion maximizes the walk's theological benefits. Discussion prompts can be used to spur theological reflection.

The first set of prompts focuses on individual sounds:

- Make a list of each sound you heard on the soundwalk.
- Which of these sounds do you consider to be sacred? Does everyone in the group agree?

- Did you hear God during the soundwalk? What did God sound like?
- Where was this soundscape noisy? In other words, at what places did you find it hard to hear yourself? To hear God? What sounds seemed to drown out your voice or God's voice?
- What sounds most surprised you? Can you describe these sounds using theological or spiritual words?

One way to deepen theological reflection is to shift attention from individual sounds heard on a soundwalk to an exploration of how sounds move, dance, and sing together. The second set of prompts focuses on acoustic *relationships* in the listening environment:

- Consider the individual sounds you listed. Imagine these sounds as parts of a musical composition. How do these sounds work together? Do any of the sounds seem to compete with one another? Does the competition add to or detract from the musical quality of the composition?
- What is the relationship of this congregation's voice to other sounds in the environment? Which sounds do we harmonize with most effectively? Which sounds are our most intimidating competitors?
- Can we choose two sounds from the walk with which we would like to have greater harmony or dialogue? Can we name some examples from the Bible where similar sounds are in harmony or dialogue?
- Try answering the above questions as though you were a teenager; a retired person; the owner of the Mexican grocery store down the street; the city council representative for your district. How does this change your responses?
- What kind of voice do we think God is calling our congregation to have on this soundscape? Describe it using vivid language. What are some biblical foundations for this kind of proclamatory voice? What can we do to develop that kind of voice?

Remembering Historical Soundmarks

Along with the soundwalk and theological reflection following the walk, a congregation may want to spend some time remembering historical soundmarks. Questions to guide this third part of the theological listening exercise might include:

- Where are peaks in sounds on the soundscape today?
- How have the peaks changed over time? Can we map these changes on a soundscape "score" that reflects our congregation's or neighborhood's acoustic story?
- Whose voices and what other sounds did the peaks primarily represent when the church was founded? Twenty years ago? Ten years ago? Five years ago?
- Which sounds do we consider sacred? Which do we want to encourage or preserve?
- Where do we want to see new peaks? How can we encourage these new peaks?

Listening into the Future

Remembering historical soundmarks is a helpful way to respect a congregation's past. Remembering also provides jumping-off places for imagining and composing future gospel soundmarks.

The following exercise can guide congregations as they use a soundwalk to listen into the future:

- Describe your congregation and its ministries as a type of musical composition (orchestral, improvisational, choral, instrumental, call and response, and so on). What characteristics are central to this musical type? Where do you hear these characteristics in your congregation's ministries?
- Describe the acoustical environment of the neighborhood as a type of musical composition. How is this description similar to or different from the description of the congregation?
- What characteristics from each musical type are important to ministry today? What are this congregation's growing acoustical edges?
- What sounds do we most need to acknowledge and to appreciate?

- Whose voices do we need to invite into our congregation's acoustical environment? What will it take for us to invite those voices? What are the risks?

Through theological reflection on soundwalking, congregations and leaders become more aware of their roles as past, present, and future gospel soundmakers.

They also become aware of their responsibility to cultivate healthy soundscapes within congregational walls and beyond. This responsibility requires competent and generous listening.

Competent and Generous Listening

"Can you help me hear God's voice?" Awash in a turbulent sea of voices and words, many people today strain their ears for sounds of God and gospel grace. For these people, echoes of God's grace are stabilizing soundmarks. This means that proclamation, or giving voice to the gospel, is a vital part of congregational ministries today. Given this, it may be surprising that the most effective gospel *proclaimers* are also good *listeners*. In other words, good *listening* is at the heart of effective Gospel *proclaiming*.

In fact, good listening is equally important and challenging to all congregations regardless of size or other distinguishing characteristics. Thus, particularly stiking in a growth economy like ours, smaller congregations like Southside Avenue Church, though struggling numerically and financially, are therefore especially equipped to model good listening skills. This is because healthy listening begins with and nurtures healthy relationships. Because of their sizes (fewer than 100 in worship), congregations like that at Southside Avenue are in a good position to cultivate healthy relationships.

One reason smaller congregations are in a good position to nurture healthy relationships and good listening skills is that healthy relationships are, first and foremost, face-to-face relationships. Face-to-face relationships demand that we embrace the theological idea that all persons are created in the sound of God and allow that idea to motivate competent and generous listening. Smaller congregations are communities unto themselves where members typically know most other members by name. Also, the effectiveness of small church ministries depends on the participation and involvement of each member. These levels of knowing and involvement characterize face-to-face relationships.

Carol Gilligan underscores the relationship between listening and healthy relationships in her classic work, *In a Different Voice: Psychological Theory and Women's Development*: "To have a voice is to be human. To have something to say is to be a person. But speaking depends on listening and being heard; it is an intensely relational act. . . . By voice I mean something like what people mean when they speak of the core of the self. Voice is natural and also cultural. It is composed of breath and sound, words, rhythm, and language. And voice is a powerful psychological instrument and channel, connecting inner and outer worlds."[3]

Speaking Depends on Listening and Being Heard

How do congregations nurture relationships grounded in this proclamatory principle of listening and being heard? How do congregations develop practices of conversation that respect all persons as being created in the sound of God? What steps can congregations take to establish more deliberate connections between everyday talk, sacred conversation, and gospel proclamation?

Writing for the corporate world, Stephen Zades and Jane Stephens describe "transformational conversation" in *Mad Dogs, Dreamers, and Sages: Growth in the Age of Ideas*.[4] Words like *transformation* and *turning together* in Zades and Stephens's writing sound strangely like theological words. In fact, the authors quote a clergyperson, Nancy Beach, to illustrate what they mean by these words. The quote reveals insights about sacred conversation: " 'I used to believe that ministry is what you did after you finished all your difficult conversations; now I realize that ministry *is* the difficult conversations. And that who I am is, to some extent, a result of all those difficult conversations.' Innovators don't *present* themselves in conversation, they *become* themselves."[5]

How do pastoral leaders and congregations engage healthfully in ministry's difficult conversations so that they and others "become themselves"?

Three characteristics of healthy conversation are keys:

> • Conversation is a multiway street. For transforming conversations to occur, all participants must commit to listening and

speaking. All participants must commit to honoring *all* voices. **Key theological assumption:** All people are created in the sound of God. Hearing God's voice in its fullness means being open to the voices of others, even voices different from ours.

• Healthy conversation and *respectful curiosity* go hand in hand. People interested in transformation enter conversations with a desire not to judge or critique but to learn from others and to discover along with them truths about God, life, and faith. **Key theological assumption:** Being open to learning about God means making oneself vulnerable to change. Really listening to others opens the door to personal transformation of ideas, beliefs, values, and behaviors.

• Conversation that changes ideas and lives needs a *safe container* in which to grow. People need a safe place to give voice to their hopes and fears. **Key assumption:** We take a risk when we offer ourselves in face-to-face conversation. But to be a risk taker is to model our lives after Jesus' life of graceful risk taking.

Zades and Stephens write that "conversation is the best tool we have for managing ideas and galvanizing the resources to turn them into action."[6] Likewise, *sacred* conversation is the best tool congregations have for hearing God's voice anew and turning that new hearing into energy for building bridges between themselves and their neighborhoods.

Put another way, God's grace calls for human response. God's grace also sets human voices free to respond. When we respond in faith, we contribute to a gracious conversation. We "contribute creatively to the exciting story of God."[7]

Conversation is rare and precious in a world saturated with words and sounds. Congregations and pastoral leaders who invest time and energy to make their churches "sounding places" for healthy conversation give their communities and the world an enormous gift.

Dynamic Gospel Proclaiming

Words and sounds flood congregational soundscapes, but *dynamic* conversation and proclamation are not heard often enough. Too frequently our conversations and gospel proclamations reside in lackluster language neighborhoods. In these neighborhoods, streets are lined with cardboard phrases, each phrase blandly alike, each insufficient to house the thoughts and feelings they were constructed to hold.

Arthur Plotnik writes about this conundrum in *The Elements of Expression*. Too often, he laments, those things we want most to tell each other escape our mouths in words that seem puny compared to the energy of thoughts or feelings that generated them.

Plotnik makes a point appropriate to congregational conversation. Ideas and beliefs trumpet with world-shaking conviction in our heads and hearts. But our words sometimes neither trumpet nor herald. To borrow a phrase from novelist Sandra Cisneros, "what is bumping like helium balloons at the ceilings of [our] brains never finds its way out. It bubbles and rises, it gurgles in the throat, it rolls across the surface of the tongue, and erupts from the lips—a belch."[8] When it comes to theology and the sacred, we often struggle to find adequate words.

The lack of spirit or passion in the words we use to describe our experiences is not necessarily due to a lack of excitement about the experience itself. Rather, our words, even those we speak with great honesty, sometimes lack what Plotnik calls "elements of force."[9] Elements of force in our speaking are vital when situations call for more than "stock phrases."

What are elements of force? They are those lively linguistic frequencies that spice up vocalizations when "the moment arrives to express the extraordinary, to achieve self expression, to pierce resistant minds."[10] Elements of force are those vocalizations that add allure to what we communicate. They replace cardboard phrases with linguistic architectural and acoustic delights that radiate energy and invite listeners to lend their ears. Such proclamations are vital to effective gospel proclamation.

Homiletician Brad Braxton puts it this way: "The news that a preacher broadcasts is so destiny-altering that it demands a passionate presentation."[11] Braxton uses words like *enthusiastic* and *extravagant* to describe how God gives God's grace to us. Preaching, Braxton insists, should also be enthusiastic and extravagant, both in its use of language and in its spiritual energy.

The same is true of our sacred conversations. God's gift in Christ is extravagant. Our conversations about that gift should be enthusiastic and extravagant. What does this mean? People committed to sacred conversation are called to infuse both their listening and their speaking with positive energy. The roots of this energy are found in healthy personal identity and spiritual awareness. When we are anointed by God's Spirit to set free our voices, we are also anointed to be passionate in the expression of those voices.

Again, an observation from Plotnik is helpful. Finding one's authentic voice, he notes, does not entail a straight line from a clearly designated here to a clearly designated there. No single template exists for twenty-first-century ministry as proclamation. Likewise, no single voice is any person's bona fide or most authentic voice: "We rarely *find* our real voice, plumbing the depths until we snare one that sounds right. Our voice can be a new voice—or several—that we *make* real, a voice in harmony with our roots but capable of expressing the full flower of the evolving self. Like everything that breaks from the ordinary, the new voice entails risks, apprehensions, missteps. These are reasonable costs of liberation."[12]

As Plotnik suggests, we speak with many voices: public, private, casual, formal. Speaking with many voices does not brand us as phony chameleons. Rather, we model the speech of people we respect. For example, we take on the dialects of our grandparents. Or we develop speech patterns for our eclectic travels from boardroom table to kitchen table. The voices that spill out of our identities at these tables reflect daily struggles to make sense of our lives and adapt to our world. As we mature, guided by our values and beliefs, these voices seek a harmony that expresses who we are.[13]

Spicing up our usual smorgasbord of expression may help to revitalize sacred conversation and gospel proclamation. The following are guidelines for conversation revitalization:

- When talking, *say what you mean*, at least to the extent that you know what you mean.
- *Use high-energy verbs* to give life to "saying what you mean."
- Let the *natural rhythms* of your speech add texture to what you say.
- *Soak up new words* to give new life to your vocabulary.
- *Take risks* of trying new ways to express yourself and your experiences of God and faith.

Reenergizing gospel proclamations based on these guidelines is important whether the new energy flows into everyday talk or the pulpit.

A Word to Preachers

The peculiarities of pulpit proclamation give rise to a few comments specific to preachers. Pastoral leaders who want to encourage a collaborative understanding of ministry as proclamation face a particular challenge. On the one hand, these leaders collaborate with congregants in a commitment to sacred conversation. This requires maintaining healthy relationships with others. It also means leading out of a collaborative understanding of pastoral authority.

On the other hand, embracing collaborative approaches to proclamation does not mean that pastoral leaders relinquish their call and responsibility to be prophets who herald God's radical message of freedom. Carol Gilligan describes teenage girls who, for the sake of "relationships," alter their ways of speaking. They alter their voices, caught between the desire to speak frankly and fearlessly and the even keener desire to remain in relationships with their peers.[14]

The challenge can be significant—to stay connected to others *and* persistently and prophetically proclaim the gospel. But learning to face that challenge and faithfully offer one's voice to gospel proclamation is an important part of what it means to be called to preach.

PART 2

Ministry as Formation

C H A P T E R   3

A   G o d   W h o
M a k e s   a n d
F o r m s

Then the LORD God formed man [adam] from the dust of the
ground, and breathed into his [adam's] nostrils the breath of life;
and the man [adam] became a living being. (Genesis 2:7)

Once upon a time, the very first once upon a time, the "earth was a formless void" (Genesis 1:2). Then God spoke. Sounds tumbled out of God's mouth, transforming emptiness into a lyrical soundscape. Sea waves splashed. Birds cooed. In the beginning, God's words gave birth to life. Or so the creation story in Genesis goes.

But Genesis actually recounts two creation stories, one in Genesis 1 and one in Genesis 2, and these two tales of beginnings narrate more than God's creation of the music of the spheres. In the Genesis 2 story, for example, divine eyes see in earth's clay the shape of humankind. Divine hands knead the clay, giving it human form. Divine breath blows into the clay the breath of life. *Adam* becomes a living creature. In the Genesis 2 story, divine fingerprints on a human vessel become the opening script for the story of human life.

Ministry as formation, like ministry as proclamation, begins with a story, a Genesis-like story about God creating human life. Rooted in Genesis' sacred beginnings story, ministry as formation relies on several theological insights:

- People discover meaning for their lives when they hear their stories *in God's story.*
- People are transformed when they embrace God's story *as their own story.*
- Congregations are called to be sounding places where God's story can unfold in people's lives.

Ministry, much like the creation stories in Genesis 1 and 2, encompasses more than sounds and words. It is about more than proclamation. In the Genesis 1 version of the creation story, God proclaimed: " 'Let there be light'; and there was light"(Genesis 1:3). In the Genesis 2 version, God "formed [*adam*] from the dust of the ground" (Genesis 2:7). God is a Creator who proclaims and forms.

This chapter explores *ministry as formation.* In particular, the chapter focuses on narrative as a primary characteristic of ministry as formation.

What Is Formation?

Ministry as Formation

To form something, *The New Webster's Encyclopedia of Dictionaries* reports, is "to give shape" to it. *Formation* is "the act of forming."[1]

Pottery making comes to mind. Potters have a goal—to give shape to amorphous clay. Skilled potters' hands form mud into pitchers, jars, or pots. On potters' wheels, lumps of clay become vessels used for eating, drinking, and serving.

But "useful" and "functional" are inadequate descriptors for potters' clay creations. Potters shape "pots of purpose."[2] But potters also give vessels artistic shapes or forms. They shape pots of beauty.

Potter Robin Hopper writes this about his identity as a potter: "Part of being a potter lies in balancing the purely practical with the purely aesthetic.... To work to the extent of one's capability and at the same time grow and flourish, one has to ... strike one's own balance."[3] In pottery making, "function" and "form" refer to practical and aesthetic aspects of a potter's work. Potters seek balance between the practical and the aesthetic in the pots they create.

How do these insights about pottery making relate to ministry as formation? Ministry as formation is the act of forming the spiritual, theological, and ethical identities of individuals and congregations. Two questions animate this shaping process:

1. Who *are* we as people of faith?
2. What are we to *do* as people of faith?

Potters shape pots that have aesthetic form and practical function. "Form" and "function," being and doing, are also foci of ministry as formation.

Put another way, ministry as formation integrates the aesthetic and practical in individual and communal faith identities. It integrates faith's *being* and *doing* elements. In fact, ministry as formation challenges the notion that being and doing reside in the separate categories into which we often put them.

Ministry as formation also invites individuals and congregations to live to the "extent of their capabilit[ies]" and to "grow and flourish."[4] Consider this example. A youth minister talks with a high school senior about future plans: "What do you want to do with your life? What gifts do you have?" These are formation questions.

What stirs formation questions like these? Most people envision productive careers. They have what some artists call a "big idea" for their lives.[5] They want to develop useful life skills. They want to shape gifts and life dreams into vocational paths.

But "useful" and "productive" alone do not characterize human desires or identities any more than they characterize a potter's creations. People seek what to do with their lives. But they also want to know that their lives have meaning beyond life's many "doings."

Thus, that same high school senior may also look in a mirror and ask herself: "Who am I? What is my life really all about?" Or a nursing home resident may wonder after eight decades of living: "What does my life mean now? What has it meant?" These questions, voiced by a teenager or a nursing home resident, are also formation questions.

Both "doing" and "being" questions point to why some people engage in leadership or spiritual formation as part of their search for a good career path. Through these formation processes and others, people work to shape their identities as human beings as part of their vocational search. What they often learn is that their identities amalgamate the aesthetic and the practical. Human being and human doing are inseparable.

To engage in ministry as *formation* is to explore life's beauty and shape life's usefulness. To engage in ministry as formation is to enter into integrative processes that reveal and shape faith identities.

Congregations and Ministry as Formation

God calls congregations to be God's people and to do God's work, in other words, to identities of being and doing. But societal needs and congregational identities take on different forms in different historical eras and sociocultural locations. Thus, congregations face an ongoing challenge to discern the shape of their identities as church for particular times and places.

To explore congregational identity is to explore from a communal perspective two questions not unlike the more individualized formation questions above:

1. Who *are* we as God's church?
2. What are we to *do* as God's church?

These are questions of *congregational* being and doing.

Congregations flourish when being and doing are in sync. In other words, congregations thrive when their sense of who they are harmonizes with their decisions and actions. But sometimes congregations lose sight of the connection between identity and action. This can lead to lethargy and disillusionment. It can also lead to conflict.

Consider Southside Avenue Church. Members cherish their identity as "church," but they are unclear about what this identity compels them to do in a changing neighborhood. They are struggling to understand who they are in the particular time and place in and to which they are called to do God's work. They may not realize it, but they are struggling to uncover the authentic core of their twenty-first-century identity.

Ministry as formation taps into the arts of storytelling and story-listening to create a healthier partnership between congregational identity and action.

Pastoral Leaders and Ministry as Formation

Congregational formation affects pastoral formation. Likewise, pastoral formation affects congregational formation. Pastoral leaders, like congregations, wrestle to balance identity and action. Again, Southside Avenue Church is an example. Andrea, as pastoral leader, struggles to balance her call to pastoral responsibilities with her call to be a person of faith. The two—pastoral doing and being—are entwined. Southside Avenue needs a leader skilled in tasks of ministry such as preaching, pastoral care, teaching, budgeting, and administrating. But a holistic sense of self depends on Andrea's ability to take time away from ministry's many tasks.

Andrea needs time to explore the rhythms of her own identity. She needs space to reflect on her own ideas and convictions about ministry. Balance is vital to her spiritual well-being and vitality as a pastoral leader.

Ministry as formation taps into the arts of storytelling and story-listening to create a healthier partnership between pastoral being and doing.

Why Storytelling and Story-listening?

Ministry as formation taps into the arts of storytelling and story-listening to create healthier partnerships between congregational and pastoral being and doing. But why storytelling?

One reason is the pervasiveness of storytelling in daily life. "Narrative is everywhere," organizational theorist Daniel Keogh writes. Stories are "as natural as the trees in the forest," Keogh writes about the relationship between narrative and healthy organizations, but his conviction about the "raw power" of stories is more far-reaching.[6]

Consider the number of stories people tell just to make it through an eight-hour workday. Or what about television programs that spike weekly ratings because their storytelling techniques entice or excite? People's lives are full of stories.

But storytelling is about more than tales recounted at the office water fountain or narratives videotaped for reality TV. Why are people enchanted by stories? Why do people tell stories so often and with so much passion? More important to our discussion, why do the arts of story-telling and story-listening reside at the core of ministry as formation?

Andrea's formation as a pastoral leader illustrates one response. The Genesis 1 creation story captured Andrea's imagination when she was five years old. A favorite aunt was the first to tell Andrea the biblical story of creation. Andrea has never forgotten her aunt's provocative front-porch narration of how God filled heaven and earth with stars, rocks, trees, flowers, and giraffes.

Over time, the Genesis 1 and 2 creation *soundscapes,* both the biblical versions and her aunt's version, became an integrated *storyscape* that enlivened and continues to enliven Andrea's identity as a pastoral leader and person of faith. Years of biblical study after those front porch narrations, Andrea has a deeper understanding of the Hebrew dialect that recounts the Genesis story. She also has a deeper understanding of how her aunt's story and the ancient Hebrew story collaborate in her theology and ministry.

Now, as a pastoral leader, Andrea eavesdrops on the stories in Genesis 1 and 2 from several vantage points. From her listening post as Southside Avenue Church's pastoral leader, Andrea hears the opening verses of Genesis 1 spin out an amazing "once upon a time." In this poetic rendition of life's beginnings, God speaks into primeval chaos and initiates a mythic tale of creation. God's voice stories life into existence.

A more scholarly reading of the two creation stories in Genesis 1 and 2, explored from her vantage point as a student of Hebrew, reminds Andrea that God creates by speaking. Proclamation and creation are inseparable in God's identity. This means that proclamation and action are inseparable. When God speaks, something happens.

Biblical scholar Walter Brueggemann expands on this. Divine proclamation and action, Brueggemann writes, together fashion a world made hospitable by God's "will and capacity to evoke and sustain life."[7] At least, this is one interpretation of the ancient Hebrew story, an interpretation made familiar to Andrea through her study of Genesis as a ministry student.

Shaped by her life's multiple perspectives on Genesis 1 and 2, Andrea's pastoral identity is characterized by a conviction that God's story of creative hospitality and innovative goodness persists. Thus, she bends her ear to catch bits and pieces of the Genesis story in the stories people tell about their lives, values, and commitments. She also listens for themes of the Genesis story in Southside Avenue Church's story.

By doing this, Andrea keeps alive her aunt's story and nurtures her own story as a person of faith, student of biblical theology, and pastoral leader. She embodies her belief that an ancient, sacred creation story is still being told today through people's beliefs and actions. She also lives out a healthy respect for "front porch" wisdom and theology. Finally, she is compelled to remind herself and congregants of the need to establish a more robust connection between word and action in Southside Avenue's ministries. Thus, stories and storytelling continue to be important to Andrea's formation as a person of faith and pastoral leader.

Other, broader reasons exist for the value of stories to ministry as formation. For example, stories enable individuals and communities to preserve memories and transmit meanings. Stories also instill values and build community.

How do stories accomplish this? Stories are creative, and storytelling is creative work. Consider the Genesis example again. The Genesis creation stories tell of *divine* creative work. But the fact that the Genesis stories are *written* accounts points to the power and potential of *human* creative work. People create narratives like Genesis to interpret life's meanings. Human storytelling is creative, interpretive work.

Sociologist Arthur Frank puts it another way. Through storytelling, he writes in *The Wounded Storyteller*, people create and recreate themselves.[8] Through storytelling, people also create and re-create their communities.

The Genesis creation narratives are biblical examples of the meaning-making capacity of stories. Illness stories provide additional examples. Frank talks about the power of illness stories. Illness, he writes, results in the loss of the "destination and map"[9] that previously guided a person's life. Illness interrupts the stories people are living. It also interferes with the stories people hope to tell in the future.

Consider the woman who survives breast cancer. Or the child injured in an automobile accident. When illnesses or injuries like these strike, chaos erupts. In fact, the chaos of illness and injury not only interrupts ongoing life stories but also leaves people with countless questions, fears, and uncertainties: "Will I have to live from now on wondering if the cancer has come back?" "When I go back to school, will I still have friends?"

For those caught up in the interruptive chaos of illness and the complexity of medical systems, storytelling can be healing and redemptive. Frank explains that when people's bodies are wounded, they receive medical care. A chief medical aim is physical healing. Storytelling taps into other healing sources. When the woman with breast cancer is given a chance to tell her story *and be heard,* a transformation occurs. She becomes what Frank calls a "wounded storyteller."[10] She becomes an active participant in her healing.

As storyteller instead of disease victim, the woman thus becomes a subject in her illness story, even though that story may be confusing and painful. Transformed into wounded but courageous storytellers, Frank emphasizes, people "recover the voices that illness and its treatment often take away."[11] They recover the ability to proclaim something meaningful about their lives.

Some of what Frank writes about illness stories applies to congregational stories. Hurting congregations sometimes rely on empirical models to resolve problems.[12] When congregations can learn to move away from the falsely tidy categories of models and pay closer attention to their own stories as part of God's story, a shift in energy and perspective occurs. Hope and health can even be restored when congregations learn to "tell" who they are as people called to embody God's grace.

That is why storytelling and story-listening are artful collaborators in ministry as formation. Stories are compelling communicators. Stories also tackle questions of identity that bewilder many congregations. The story of Mountain View Church narrates an example.

The Story of Mountain View Church: An Example

Clues to values *and* behaviors are embedded in the clay of congregational stories. Ministry as formation searches out those clues. Ministry as formation also shapes and reshapes the clay of congregational stories into more *meaning*-ful and *purpose*-ful vessels.

Robert is Mountain View Church's pastoral leader. Andrea met Robert at a leadership workshop. Robert told her part of Mountain View's story.

Mountain View Church is seventy-five years old. Farmers and factory workers built the church brick by brick as they could afford it. Even now, the church is a communal reminder of the way things used to be.

But though the church stands in the community as a historical landmark, the community is no longer the way it used to be. Each year urban development sprawls closer to Mountain View. Farmers age. Their children move away. The agricultural economy declines.

Robert accepted a pastoral call to Mountain View Church three years ago. He struggles to understand who Mountain View Church was, who it is, and who it can become. He also struggles to understand who he is as pastoral leader in relation to this beleaguered church.

Recently, Robert guided Mountain View through a planning process in which members conceived a descriptive caption for a new church sign: *"We are the place and face of God in this community."* The church treasurer summarized the caption's meaning. "When people drive by," she explained, "they see our church and know that God is being worshiped here and has been worshiped here for almost a hundred years."

The place and the face of God in this community. The caption rings true. Rugged farmers' faces mirror the church's decades-long commitment to

God and the community. In fact, commitment and stubborn toughness are as much a part of the building as mortar and wooden beams. The faith of Mountain View Church members is planted deep in the soil of the place called Mountain View.

Still, Robert and other church leaders fear for Mountain View Church's future. Attendance is dwindling, and shrinking finances are a constant concern. How can Mountain View Church, the place and face of God in the community, draw new faces to its doors?

No clear answer to this question has surfaced in council meetings. But an insight emerged at the leadership workshop when a colleague made an observation: "The *visual* image of the 'face' is nice. The caption makes me see the church. But what does Mountain View Church *sound* like? How do people hear God's voice there?"

Robert and Andrea continue to mull over this observation. Both Mountain View and Southside Avenue churches are enduring *visual* reminders of Christian faith in their communities. They are religious landmarks, historic "places of God." But how can they grow into the gospel call to be places people today associate with the face *and* sound of God? How can they rediscover their voices as timeless and timely gospel proclaimers?

Ministry as formation asks questions like these. Congregations can pose the questions even more succinctly:

- What is the gospel for this time in this place?
- What does this gospel call us to do as God's church?

Storytelling and story-listening tease out responses that can lead to healthy practices of ministry as formation.

We turn now to the first question: *What is the gospel for this time in this place?*

What Is the Gospel? Stories and Theology

What is the gospel? The gospel is a story. More specifically, in the New Testament's four recorded Gospel narrations (Matthew, Mark, Luke, and John), we encounter not one, but four renderings of Jesus' life story. Could the gospel be a compilation of many stories?

For Christians, regardless of our response to this question, the gospel is sacred story. Religion professor Robert McAfee Brown writes that the gospel is "the Story."[13] Put another way, the gospel is the story that Christian congregations proclaim as their core defining story.

Brown uses the example of liberation theology to illustrate the power of "the Story." Liberation theologies emerged in the second half of the twentieth century among oppressed Latino and Latina people. In liberation theologies, Brown explains, "the contemporary story and 'The Story' are heard as part of *the same story*, and cannot be disengaged." For people who daily face poverty and oppression, "The Story" is a life-giving "way of telling *their* story, and, in the process, it becomes a vehicle of liberation."[14]

This example from liberation theologies underscores what Brown sees as a vital question for Christian theology and ministry: How can the Christian story be proclaimed such that listeners respond with recognition, "That's my story too"? A different version of this question may also be important: Can individual and congregational stories also be lived, remembered, and told in such a way that listeners respond with recognition, "That's the gospel story too"?

Narrative theologians improvise on this theme.[15] Like Brown, they focus on the narrative character of Christian faith. Individuals are transformed, narrative theologians emphasize, when they embrace God's story in Christ as their own.

To summarize, two questions shape ministry as formation's work of connecting stories and theology:

1. How can the Christian story be proclaimed so that listeners respond with the recognition, "That's my story too"?
2. Can individual and congregational stories also be lived, remembered, and told in such a way that listeners respond with recognition, "That's the gospel story too"?

We turn briefly to the second of these two questions.

The Sacredness of Personal Stories

A gift congregations can offer people is to invite them to "tell us your story." What makes this invitation a gift? It implies a promise: "We will listen." In a sound-deluged world, such a promise is rare: "Your voice and story are valuable. We want to hear you. God wants to hear you." To offer such a gift, congregations have to consider carefully what stories they deem part of their sacred canon.

What is a *canon*? A theological definition says that the "canon" is the "writings, as books of the Bible, considered holy or authoritative."[16] The Bible contains the official collection of writings deemed holy by church authorities when the Bible was canonized. The official biblical canon has sustained Christian communities for centuries, wielding enormous power in Christian history, both for good and ill. It demands our attention today.

In fact, one type of narrative theology is called "canonical narrative theology." Canonical narrative theologians, theologian Heather Walton writes, consider the story of Jesus "a divinely authorized narrative in which the truth concerning human history is made evident."[17] People become Christian, canonical theologians insist, as they learn to play their parts in the sacred narrative of Jesus.

But what if the New Testament's example of four Gospel renderings paves the way for expanded narrative attentiveness? Perhaps the gospel is not one story but many stories. Perhaps the gospel even contains stories not found in the biblical canon.

Katie Cannon, a black feminist theologian, is judged "a brave practitioner of human archaeology" largely because of her commitment to this expanded attentiveness.[18] Cannon explores black women's literature as sacred texts. Examples of the kinds of stories Cannon deems sacred are slave narratives, imaginative literature and poetry, autobiographies, and testimonies of black churchwomen.

Cannon invites us to hear these stories as connected to the *official* sacred canon. She also invites us to listen to these stories as sacred rhetoric. This sacred rhetoric, she insists, chronicles the faith and courage that shaped and continues to shape African American communities: "In their plots, actions, and depictions of characters, Black women writers flesh out the positive attributes of Black folks who are 'hidden beneath the ordinariness of everyday life.' They also plumb their own imaginations in order to crack the insidiousness of worn-out stereotypes. . . . Black women's literature offers the sharpest available view of the Black community's soul."[19] Cannon's theological work reminds us that the official Christian canon, the Bible, does not contain every sacred story. Nor does the written record of Christian or even human history.

Walton's description of "constructive" narrative theology echoes this. In constructive forms of narrative theology, she writes, "it is in the human capacity for storytelling itself, rather than in a pre-existing grand narrative, that redemptive power is located."[20] Storytelling constructs meaning. Storytelling shapes human lives and faith.

Thus, Cannon invites us to remain open to stories that may contain unexplored wisdom about God. She challenges us to listen to the "noncanonical other" as sacred storyteller. But she flags this work with a warning. This work, Cannon writes, "is difficult work. It is unglamorous, incremental, unsentimental, often invisible. It demands vigilance and courage, and it must be lubricated by humor."[21]

Both Walton's and Cannon's insights point to an important connection between narrative theology and ministry as formation. If we want to discover the gospel anew for today's diverse contexts, previously unheard voices and their stories need places to "sound" along with louder, more familiar voices. Congregations and pastoral leaders, along with Cannon, need to become skilled practitioners of human archaeology. Ministry as formation is energized as congregations learn to listen for and value the sacred, the gospel story, in each person's unfolding life story.

Congregations as Sacred Sounding Places

A distant locomotive whistles in the night. We hear the sound and remember a childhood home.

A firefighter stands at Ground Zero in New York City on Memorial Day 2005. The city's familiar sounds hum and buzz around her. But in her heart echo the sounds of September 11, 2001—sirens, shouts, and weeping.

A Ford Mustang's muffler rumbles. Grandma's and Grandpa's eyes twinkle. For each, the mind's eye sees again that first-date picnic spot and the Ford that carried them there forty-eight years ago.

All places, like these examples, are "sounding." People associate sounds and places. As we saw in chapters 1 and 2, many people seek places where they can hear the sounds of God. They seek places where they can listen to and reflect on the sounds of their own voices. They seek places where they can make sense of the world's deluge of sounds and where they can hear each other. They also seek places where they can let their voices go into the ears of trustworthy listeners.

Ministry as formation empowers congregations to become *trustworthy* sounding places where people can listen for God and discover the storytelling sounds of their voices. Congregations can ask themselves several questions as they embrace this vocational responsibility:

- Who is valued as a storyteller here?
- Is our congregation a safe container for people's stories?
- How do we respect individual stories *and* fashion a shared congregational story?

God calls congregations to *be* sacred sounding places for human and divine stories. This call to *being* is simultaneously a call to *doing*. Thus, we move to a second question central to healthy congregational practices of ministry as formation: *What does this gospel story call us to do?*

What Are We to Do as God's Church? Story and Action

God calls congregations to be God's people and to do God's work. God calls congregations to actions of justice and care. These actions of justice and care are shaped and nurtured within the storytelling dimensions of ministry as formation.

Story-Shaped Communities of Action

Ministry as formation invites congregations to listen with greater attentiveness to their communal stories, both the stories they tell and the stories they live. Ministry as formation also encourages congregations to tell and live their stories with greater depth and dimension. In other words, ministry as formation nurtures story-shaped communities of action.

Mountain View Church again provides an example. Mountain View may not have a full-bodied public voice at this time in its history, but Robert experiences a wealth of storytelling skill and energy in members' everyday lives.

What about retired church members who claim a table each morning at a local restaurant? The stories they tell over coffee entertain listeners *and* build relationships. Or what about long-time church friends who spend time each year preserving homegrown blackberries? As they preserve berries, they also preserve important life moments through storytelling and story-listening.

Everyday stories like these underscore the power of storytelling to forge friendships and create community. Some everyday stories told and embodied by church members also announce the gospel. For example, Robert is certain he heard the gospel as two farmers swapped tomato-planting stories. Whether the farmers realized it or not, their storytelling and story-listening were about more than tomatoes, for in sharing gardening stories, they tapped into memories of that time when one farmer tilled the other's garden during several months of cancer treatments.

Or what about a story Mountain View's pianist narrates? When the pianist was in the hospital, a church member, Alena, visited her. Alena sits on a back pew each Sunday and rarely talks to anyone. But she visited the hospital. The pianist loves to tell the story: "Alena, when you visited that afternoon, you looked just like God to me." Again, Robert heard the gospel as ninety-year-old Alena and the pianist unexpectedly enacted the reconciling dialogue between Esau and Jacob narrated in a familiar Genesis story (see Genesis 33:10).

Gospel truths contained in congregational story vessels like these are often subtle and can be hard to hear in a world that more boisterously heralds other kinds of news. They can also be hard to hear when congregations amplify particular stories over others.

Sometimes, for example, a "larger-than-life" congregational hero story can grow to proportions that overshadow other congregational stories. In congregations where this happens, particular story lines become dominant while others are suppressed or de-emphasized. In these dominant story lines, certain characters become legendary. By contrast, other characters are cast primarily as backdrops to the character deemed "hero," or particular characters are assigned roles of victim or villain so that the hero can remain heroic. Sometimes congregants feel pressure to tell their own stories to fit into the dominant story line. One result can be that congregational values and self-understanding gravitate toward one-dimensionality and gospel possibilities of other story lines are lost.

Questions like the following may help congregations pay more careful attention to the way they tell their communal stories of gospel identity and action:

- What story does a congregation tell as its greatest "success" story and who are the main characters in this story?
- Who are the main characters in a congregation's "birth" story?
- What is a congregation's most remembered and retold "crisis" story and who are the primary characters in this story?
- What kinds of stories does a congregation rarely tell?
- What biblical stories and characters are most recognizable in a congregation's stories?

Posing questions like these is one way to encourage congregations to listen more attentively to all of their stories.

To listen more attentively is to liberate overshadowed or ignored stories and to tell dominant stories more realistically. To listen more attentively is also to give all congregants a chance to be subjects in their own, the congregation's, and God's unfolding stories. That is why Robert is working hard to learn the art of attentive and generous story-listening. This is no easy task because attention spans today seem to be shrinking. Also, it takes time and energy to listen to stories that continually evolve and change.

But by listening more attentively, Robert has begun to hear more tones and timbres in his own as well as Mountain View Church's story. He has also witnessed the power of stories to shape how we see ourselves, God, and others.

Restless Prophets or Patient Priests?

Congregations are called to provide consistency, continuity, and community as individuals move toward spiritual self-awareness and maturity. Congregations are also called to be sounding places where God's story and human stories meet. Both callings are vital to ministry as formation in a world where some life stories are rejected.

Ministry as formation also has a more public role. What is that public role? God calls congregations and their leaders to discern when to be *restless storytelling prophets or patient story-listening priests*.

For example, local congregations, communities, and nations wrestle with painful stories of injustice and oppression. To embody the gospel story is to resist these stories and the destructive actions that accompany them. In other words, to embody the gospel story in cases of injustice and oppression is to become prophetic voices of resistance.

Consider stories of domestic violence or racism. Destructive stories like these cry out for a kind of passionate gospel impatience. Our call as Christians is to trumpet the gospel cry of liberation and healing in the face of stories that imprison or destroy. We are restlessly to knell the gospel cry that justice be made a reality *now*.

Other stories call for patient, storytelling priests. Stories of depression illustrate this. It is hard to journey with a loved one through depression. Eager for such a painful story to reach a happier, more peaceful ending, we can become impatient listeners. But healing from depression can take a lifetime. Some stories do not have tidy endings. They call for patient listeners.

To *tell* stories is, in a sense, to tell our identities. To *listen* to stories—our own and those of others—is to listen to individual and communal identities. To invest time and energy in both acts—telling and listening—is to form and transform identities. This is the work of ministry as formation. Ministry as formation is a lifelong process of moving back and forth between story-listening and storytelling, between paying attention and creating, between canonizing and constructing. It is a lifelong process of discovering and naming connections between human stories and God's story. It is a lifelong process of discerning God's call to participate in communal stories of gospel care and grace.

The Transforming Shape of Ministry as Formation

The gospel story invites congregations to be transformed. Our own stories also invite us in this way, as do the stories of our neighbors and sometimes even of strangers. How can we hear our own stories and the stories of others and recognize "that's the gospel story too"? We turn again to the story of Mountain View Church.

One Sunday, Robert invited a friend to teach a song in sign language during the children's sermon. A few weeks later, a church member narrated to Robert a related story about Mountain View Church that revealed unexpected and liberating truths about Mountain View's gospel storytelling.

Seventy-five years ago, three families dug the first shovels of dirt for Mountain View Church's foundation. One of these families had two children. Both children had significant hearing loss. The parents learned sign language and taught it to their children. Many in the church also learned signed words and phrases.

Thus, at least some of Mountain View Church's earliest gospel *sounding* took the form of skilled hands scripting visual words onto silent landscapes. Some of Mountain View Church's early soundings were God's words "spoken" by expressive hands and faces. Ministry as formation and proclamation took the shape of sign language.

Robert was astounded as he listened. Sounds of prophetic consciousness echoed in this story. Even today persons with hearing loss and other disabilities live too often on society's political, economic, and communal margins. But Mountain View Church became a *visual* gospel story sounding place for a family facing the difficult challenges of hearing loss during the Great Depression. In this past story, the Mountain View congregation became prophet and priest in a story line of hospitality, care, and grace.

We are the place and face of God in this community. The caption at first seemed only a one-dimensional quip for a church sign. However, because he was given the gift of one of Mountain View Church's founding stories, Robert now heard the caption's historical, spiritual, and metaphorical depths.

Robert also heard a challenge. People on life's margins today thirst for hospitality and grace. They need congregational vessels that offer life-giving gospel nectar. They need safe congregational containers to hold their most sacred stories. They need support while they reflect on what it means for their voices to proclaim the gospel and their stories to embody God's grace. How can Robert lead Mountain View Church to celebrate its past story of response to these needs? Along with that, how can he encourage congregants to embody this past story's gospel truths as they fashion present and future story lines?

Ministry as formation empowers congregations to restory their lives in light of the gospel story. To undertake this liberating and life-giving work, both Mountain View and Southside Avenue churches must seek out links between God's story and the stories unfolding in their community. They must be open to putting their congregational clay on the potter's wheel to shape and reshape story-pots sturdy and resilient enough to endure contemporary chaos.

The next chapter considers some specific ideas for undertaking this formative work.

CHAPTER 4

In God's House Are Many Rooms

In [God's] house there are many dwelling places. If it were not so, would I have told you that I go to prepare a place for you? (John 14:2)

Clay for the work of ministry as formation can be found in three congregational dimensions:

1. Worship life
2. Organizational life
3. Spiritual life

This chapter contains guidelines for becoming better congregational storytellers and story-listeners, and thus more effective practitioners of ministry as formation, within each of these dimensions.

Storytelling, Story-Listening, and Worship Life

Chapter 2 explored the relationship between *proclamation* and the Lord's Table in worship. We turn now to the connection between *formation* and the Lord's Table. Several facets of worship exemplify the connections:

- *Testimonio*
- Celebrations and concerns

- Table rituals
- Narrative preaching

Testimonios

At the Lord's Table, we eat a meal and remember a story. In a sense, theologian Gerald Loughlin explains, we *absorb* a meal and a story, in particular the Lord's Meal and the gospel story. This meal and story also absorb us.[1] Loughlin puts it this way: "[Participants] are not simply witnesses of the story, but characters within it. They do not simply recall the forgiveness of sins but ask and receive forgiveness; they do not repeat the praise of others but give praise themselves; they do not merely remember the night on which Jesus was betrayed but . . . gather with the apostles at that night's table, themselves called by the one who in that darkness called his disciples to eat with him."[2] Loughlin's theological premise is that as worshipers join the disciples with Jesus around the Lord's Table, they absorb and are absorbed by meal and story.

But how are worship leaders to encourage participant awareness of these depths of meaning? Andrea glimpsed in a Latino and Latina worship service an avenue to greater awareness and, thus, to greater liturgical depth. In addition to lively praise music, *testimonios* also enlivened the worship soundscape the day Andrea visited. The Latino and Latina worship practice of *testimonios*, Andrea realized, may provide insights for worship renewal at Southside Avenue Church.

In English, *testimony* means a "solemn declaration or affirmation."[3] The Spanish word, *testimonio*, carries a similar meaning. People who share *testimonios* in worship declare, usually in story form, something about their faith. *Testimonios* link human stories and God's story.

For example, some *testimonios* in the Latino and Latina worship service that day trumpeted thanksgivings. Others lamented illnesses, job losses, or other personal struggles. A daughter celebrated her father's safe arrival in the United States from Mexico, but in the next moment expressed fear about her husband's upcoming journey: "He will cross the border by hanging onto the underside of a truck." Both kinds of *testimonios*—celebration and lament—were heard and acknowledged by other worshipers who nodded, sang choruses, or applauded in response.

Theologian Elizabeth Conde-Frazier explores *testimonios* from a mujerista, or Latina feminist, perspective. Her emphasis on silenced voices and stories echoes Katie Cannon's work, discussed in chapter 3. In particular, Conde-Frazier points to how *testimonios* shed light on the theological dimensions of everyday stories.

Through *testimonios,* everyday stories are voiced around the Lord's Table along with the gospel story. Carving out space for *testimonios* in worship, Conde-Frazier writes, "makes the doing of theology not a purely academic task but includes the voices of those who have been silenced.... Where can one find the theology of the people? It is found in *lo cotodiano*—the everyday, and is told in our stories of faith, *testimonios.*"[4] Borrowing from religious educators Margaret Ann Crain and Jack Seymour, Conde-Frazier observes that *testimonios* are the "people's theology."[5] A closer look at Crain and Seymour's work is useful at this point.

Crain and Seymour conducted interviews with laypeople to uncover how people in congregations "engage in religious knowing in everyday life."[6] People search for meaning in every aspect of their lives. Crain and Seymour use the phrase "a people's theology"[7] to refer to the work people do to connect faith with life's feelings, experiences, and commitments, in other words, with their searches for life's meaning.

To do theology healthfully, Crain and Seymour observe, people need congregations where they can "search safely" for life's meanings and purposes, even and perhaps especially in the face of "mysteries of brokenness and hope [they] cannot unravel."[8] To do theological reflection health-fully, people need places where they can make connections between everyday life and God's grace.

Though often overlooked by pastoral leaders, one aspect of a people's theology is vital to ministry as formation, Conde-Frazier explains. Everyday life *finds* meaning *in* theology. This premise forms a partial foun-dation for people's theology. The reverse, though sometimes disregarded, is also foundational. Everyday life—*lo cotodiano*—*contributes* meaning *to* theology.

For example, the Latino and Latina worship service Andrea visited gave people space through *testimonios* to unravel life's meanings *in light of* the gospel. But testimonios also revealed theological understandings *about* the gospel. Through *testimonios,* people gave voice to their stories. In doing so, they also gave voice to their theologies.

In the worship service that day, Andrea witnessed the theological power of hospitable and generous storytelling and story-listening. Letty M. Russell offers a theological definition of hospitality: "Hospitality is an expression of unity without uniformity.... Hospitality creates a safe and welcoming space for persons to find their own sense of humanity and worth."⁹ Put another way, hospitality creates safe space for storytelling and story-listening, and creates safe space where a people's theology can emerge and be cultivated.

Crain and Seymour are concerned that congregations do not always provide adequate space for people to make connections between their daily lives and faith commitments.¹⁰ Too many congregations and pastoral leaders deem theology and theological reflection the professional province of the clergy. Or they relegate theological reflection to the periphery of congregational life.

To decrease this artificial and nonproductive gap between theology and daily life, congregations like that at Southside Avenue may need to pose questions such as the following:

- Does our congregation give people a safe space to search for life's meanings in the midst of everyday feelings, commitments, and experiences?
- Does our congregation see and hear God in people's everyday stories?
- Does our congregation make space for stories told in different dialects?
- Does our congregation make space for stories that challenge familiar faith perspectives?
- Does our congregation embody gospel hospitality?

Life-giving responses are embedded in congregational clay.

Southside Avenue Church exemplifies this embeddedness. At Southside Avenue, hospitality often takes the shape of caring questions. "How are you today?" is an example of a rudimentary question of hospitality. Skilled practitioners at Southside Avenue turn asking hospitable questions like this into a ministerial art form.

For example, several members have fashioned a vibrant ministry out of remembering people's important life events. On Sundays, these members welcome people with questions that show attentive care: "How is your mother's hip?" "Did you get a chance to see your son's new home?" "How did you celebrate your anniversary?" This ministry of hospitality permeates Monday through Saturday by way of e-mail and phone calls.

These hospitable church members are teaching Andrea that to show hospitality is to pay attention to people's lives, even to seemingly mundane manifestations of hopes, fears, and passions. To show hospitality is to give amorphous cultural issues human faces and stories. To show hospitality is to open oneself to God's story as it ebbs and flows in human lives and experiences.

Testimonios and hospitality are important to ministry as formation. However, sharing testimonies is for some congregations a lost art. Homiletician Thomas G. Long proposes one reason. "The terms 'witnessing' and 'giving a testimony,'" he writes, "have often been associated with some of the more aggressive forms of evangelism.... As such, 'witness' is a good word that has gotten into some trouble through no fault of its own."[11] "Testimony," too, may merit new attention.

By incorporating storytelling and story-listening into established parts of their congregations' worship services, Andrea and other pastoral leaders can begin to reclaim healthy practices of testimony and hospitality. Worship "celebrations and concerns" provide one possibility for reclamation.

Celebrations and Concerns

Prayer is central to Christian worship. Many congregations carve out time in worship for prayers of the people. Whether called "celebrations and concerns," "petitions," or "pastoral prayers," prayers of the people are sacred storytelling and story-listening moments.

Structured liturgies can highlight the narrative dimensions of prayer. For example, questions like the following invite and guide narrative, communal prayer:

- What personal or communal events do we celebrate today?
- What global events do we celebrate or lament?
- For whom do we give thanks?
- For whom do we seek comfort or healing?
- From whom do we seek comfort or healing?

Narrative prayer liturgies can also be rooted in the day's biblical texts. If the sermon is based on the story of the Good Samaritan in Luke 10, for example, a prayer liturgy could underscore the prophetic definition of neighborliness found in that story:

- Who are our neighbors?
- When have we been good neighbors?
- What needs do our neighbors have?
- What do we need from our neighbors?
- Who has been an unexpected neighbor to us?

Prayers of the people are enlivened when worshipers are invited in worship to answer questions like these.

The intended outcome is not necessarily entire personal or communal narratives spoken aloud. But when names and concerns are vocalized by congregants and placed before God in prayer, fuller stories are at least implied. Congregational worship participation is encouraged. Also, over time, more full-bodied *testimonios* could emerge as people learn through worship's time of celebrations and concerns the art of prayerful call and response.

Table Rituals

Jesus shared meals with many people. The Gospel of Matthew testifies to Jesus' hospitable table fellowship: "The Son of Man came eating and drinking, and they say, 'Look, a glutton and a drunkard, a friend of tax collectors and sinners!'" (Matthew 11:19).

The Gospel of Luke echoes Matthew's testimony:

> One of the Pharisees asked Jesus to eat with him, and he went into the Pharisee's house and took his place at the table. (Luke 7:36)

> . . .

> All who saw it began to grumble and said, "He has gone to be the guest of one who is a sinner." (Luke 19:7)

Jesus' biblical table etiquette throughout the Gospels epitomizes hospitality. When Jesus was present at a table, people were welcomed, challenged, and changed, and their stories and voices were heard and acknowledged. People can be welcomed, challenged, and changed at sacred meal tables today. Voices and stories can be heard and acknowledged.

The following sample liturgy frames a fellowship meal and exemplifies acts of welcome and challenge. Such a liturgy invites congregations to think more theologically about fellowship meals and to embody Jesus' meal values at their tables. The liturgy also helps congregations to practice hospitable storytelling and story-listening.

Beginning the Meal

Leader:	Greetings and welcome.
Gathering:	How good it is when brothers and sisters sit together in unity!

56

Leader:	Let it be known that this is no ordinary meal!
Gathering:	What kind of meal will it be?
Leader:	This meal will not only be a time to be present together, it will also be a time to enjoy one another's presence.
Gathering:	How good it is when sisters and brothers enjoy one another's presence!
Leader:	This meal will nourish not only physical bodies but also minds and souls.
Gathering:	How good it is when brothers and sisters nourish mind and soul! We thank God. Let us eat together.[12]

The Meal

To start the meal, those gathered break and share loaves of bread available at each table, speaking together the following:

How blessed are You, Creator of the Whole,
the vast universe and those who dwell on planet Earth!
You care about us so much that you feed us
with the Bread of Life that we, in turn, may feed others.[13]

A leader can introduce questions throughout the meal to encourage storytelling. These storytelling cues can be linked to a theme. For example, the following questions might generate stories around a harvest theme:

• What are we harvesting in our individual lives this season?
• What are we are harvesting in our congregational life?
• What harvest stories do we remember from childhood?
• What stories of growing into or out of things do we remember?
• What causes us to resist spiritual growth?
• What cultivates growth?
• How can good things harvested in our congregation be shared with our neighbors?

Ending the Meal

The meal ends with a benedictory challenge to go out and live Jesus' table values when gathered at other tables.

At this point a caution is in order. Hospitality, Russell warns, has limits. Authentic, life-giving hospitality comes only from communities with a clear sense of "identity in Christ."[14] Congregations who want to practice gospel table hospitality must know who they are and what they do and do not have to share. This brings our discussion to a focus on narrative preaching.

Narrative Preaching

Jesus proclaimed the gospel through parables, in other words through a narrative. Through narrative preaching, pastoral leaders emulate Jesus' proclamatory style. Narrative preaching links human stories and the gospel story, underscoring how *lo cotodiano* (the everyday) incarnates the gospel story.

Thus, listening to people's stories in light of God's story in Scripture, and vice versa, stirs theological insight and leads to effective proclamation. The following questions can guide this kind of listening:

- What stories reside in this congregation and neighborhood?
- If congregational members were to write a novel about their life together, what would be the title of the novel? What would be the chapter headings? Who would be the main characters?
- If people in the neighborhood were to write a novel about this congregation, what would be the title of the novel? Who would our neighbors determine to be the main characters?
- How can the people in this community, with these unique stories, hear the gospel of the grace of God as it appears in the biblical story?[15] How do this congregation's stories connect with biblical stories?
- What kind of world does this congregation's story suggest we live in?
- What kind of character is God in this story? What kind of character is Jesus?

Questions like these, along with the responses they generate, suggest that one-size-fits-all templates for biblical interpretation and preaching cannot be applied to each congregational context. Homiletician Leonora Tubbs Tisdale underscores this. Congregations, she writes, are part of biblical interpretation much earlier and more deeply than the "text to theme to application" approach to preaching allows.[16] Each preaching context is different and engenders contextually different perspectives on and understandings of biblical texts.

In other words, biblical interpretations vary from one congregation to the next. To take adequate account of this in preaching requires what Tisdale calls "priestly listening" and "priestly questioning."[17] In other words, narrative preaching requires storytelling and story-listening hospitality, specifically in terms of listening to biblical texts and congregations.

Human life is parabolic. Human life is sacred story unfolding. Pastoral leaders are called to listen for that sacred story as it emerges in the peculiarities of local congregations. Pastoral leaders are also called to proclaim gospel truths that emerge as people hear their stories in God's story and claim God's story as their own. Worship life generates these opportunities of ministry as formation. *Organizational life* also generates ministry as formation.

Storytelling, Story-Listening, and Organizational Life

Andrea struggles to do pastoral work somewhere between the call to creativity and the exercise of imagination on the one hand, and the day-to-day administrative requirements of organizational life on the other. Other pastoral leaders share this struggle. "What do all of these administrative tasks have to do with my calling?" Andrea sometimes wonders.

Storytelling and story-listening stir creativity, imagination, and innovation in worship and preaching. Storytelling and story-listening can also infuse vacuous administrative tasks and organizational structures with new life.

A Southside Avenue congregational meeting became a mini-seminar on how storytelling influences organizational life. The meeting focused on a significant issue in which another denomination had asked if a Latino minister and a group of volunteers could use Southside Avenue's church building for a tutoring program.

Pros and cons shot through the discussion: "Why should we let another denomination have a mission in our church?"; "At least we would make use of the building"; "Suppose they damage the building"; "We have a hard enough time holding onto members without giving up space to another church"; "Maybe some of our members could volunteer"; "But our members either work or are in declining health"; "That denomination's theology is not the same as ours"; "Even if some children and parents from the tutoring program attend our church, our budget problems won't be solved."

Debate heated up. Conflict threatened.

But then a church member who owned a business began to tell a story: "Once when I was unable to do a job on my own, I recommended another person whose work I respect. Seems risky, I know, to think of competitors as colleagues. This competitor and I don't even go about our work the same way. But my business actually grew some after I recommended him. I think customers trust someone who cares about their needs. I don't know if an afterschool program will bring us new members, but it sure might say something about who we are. It might even say something about who we think God is."

The church member's story became a "springboard story." Corporate trainer Stephen Denning advocates springboard stories to aid organizational decision making. Springboard stories, he writes, give people energy for taking a leap in understanding or a leap in action.[18]

Southside Avenue's congregational meeting exemplifies the health-inducing possibilities of springboard stories. Once the church member had told her business story, other ideas, suggestions, and even concerns surged to the surface, only now some were expressed in story form. A different kind of energy infused the discussion, and Andrea heard congregational voices she had not heard before.

The business meeting did not resolve the issue. Debate continued. But because of two unexpected "springboard" stories, Southside Avenue Church began to listen to its identity in a different way. Both the Latino and Latina congregation's tutoring program proposal and the church member's personal experience were springboard stories into congregational identity work.

Congregational clay holds many creative but unformed ideas. Springboard stories tap into hidden dimensions of organizational creativity. Several characteristics of springboard stories make them useful decision-making partners:

- Springboard stories draw people into a different mode of knowing.[19]
- Sringboard stories move away from hierarchy toward collaboration.[20]

• Springboard stories are more interested in generating wisdom than in transferring information.[21]

Successful storytelling can spur organizations to clarify identities and values. This is important for Southside Avenue Church. Congregations sometimes lose sight of the connection between who they are and what they are called to do as God's people. Storytelling can refocus that connection.

Again, however, a caution is in order. Southside Avenue Church's story is complicated. Gospel values challenge members to reach out to their neighbors, and improved storytelling and story-listening may even inspire the church to connect with its Latino and Latina neighbors. But, as discussed in chapter 3, attendance or membership growth likely will not resolve budget problems. Also, story-based decision-making processes are energy and time consuming for pastoral leaders *and* congregations. In some circumstances, such time and energy are not available.

What a storytelling approach *can* do is recast financial questions. For example, a pastoral leader or consultant can use story-based questions like the following to preface congregational financial decision making.

• What is the dominant financial story in our congregation?
• What cultural stories form parts of our financial story?
• Are there biblical stories that might shape our future financial story?
• Do other congregations have stories that might be useful as we shape our future story?
• Where does the financial story fit in our overall congregational story? Where does it fit in the neighborhood's story?
• Has our financial story overshadowed other important congregational stories?

Denning describes several kinds of springboard stories. For example, leaders can tell stories from or about other contexts where similar issues have been faced. Such stories can function as springboards into the congregation's own story. Or leaders may decide to use biblical stories as springboards. Upon choosing and telling a biblical story, the leader can invite consideration of how the biblical story intersects with the congregational story. To take seriously this question is to engage a deep level of congregational theological reflection, thereby taking steps toward new possibilities.

The results when an organization enters a narrative doorway into finances or other organizational issues can be surprising and quite life-giving. Financial questions are not ignored. But, as stated above, they are approached from a different perspective, often a more biblical or theological perspective. Such a perspective can lead to healthier organizational lives *and* healthier spiritual lives.

Storytelling, Story-Listening, and Spiritual Life

Ministry as proclamation encourages people to claim their voices. Ministry as formation encourages people to hear their stories as part of God's story. Emma's story exemplifies both complexities and possibilities of this speaking and listening work. Emma has been a Southside Avenue Church member for forty-two years. She recently spent her seventy-first birthday in a rehabilitation center, apart from her husband of forty-eight years and away from her home. Her doctor is not sure she will be able to go back to her familiar life.

Significant, though often unvoiced, theological questions are present each time Andrea visits Emma:

- How are Emma's and God's stories connected?
- How is God's story connected to stories of countless persons who spend their older years in nursing homes?
- What stories does Emma tell about Southside Avenue?
- How are these stories related to Southside Avenue's identity?
- How are Emma's story and Southside Avenue's story connected?
- How is Emma's story connected to the stories of Southside Avenue's Latino and Latina neighbors?
- What gospel truths can the Southside Avenue congregation proclaim with authenticity about Emma and her story?

Questions like these seek responses from sometimes unyielding congregational clay. But questions like these also spark identity-forming theological reflection for Emma, Andrea, and Southside Avenue Church.

Life-giving responses, however, do not emerge from congregational clay as doctrinal shapes. Life-giving responses begin with hospitable storytelling and story-listening. Consider Emma's and Southside Avenue's stories. Emma's and Southside Avenue's stories intersect each time a church member visits Emma, or each time someone provides dinner for Emma's husband, or each time Emma's name is spoken during Sunday prayers. God's story is made concrete at these intersections. Spiritual growth is also made concrete.

At these intersections, however, a caution is again in order. Attentive story-listeners take a risk. They risk making themselves vulnerable to joy and pain in others' stories. They also risk misunderstanding and misinterpretation.

For example, even when pastoral leaders strive to listen generously, attentively, and hospitably, they do not always hear another person's story clearly or in depth. Sometimes this is because pastoral leaders lack clarity or self-awareness about their own stories, and sometimes it is because people in pain have a hard time articulating their feelings and thoughts.

Even though attentive story-listeners take a risk, however, they also open themselves to potential blessing. When people risk shared story-telling and story-listening, they open themselves to life-giving, growth-cultivating spiritual truth: we are all paragraphs in God's story; our stories are spiritually connected.

Some Concluding Thoughts

The play *Tamara* was first presented at Strachan House in Trinity-Bellwoods Park, Toronto, Ontario, Canada, on May 8, 1981.[22] The play, performed in a house with more than a dozen rooms, utilizes interactive staging that eliminates familiar divisions between audience and actors. Instead of watching the play from stationary theater seats, spectators accompany from room to room whatever character and story they choose. Spectators enter into the play as active participants.

Spectators enter even more deeply into the play as participants due to the fact that *Tamara's* multiple scenes are enacted simultaneously on stages throughout the theater. One theater critic tabulated the possible number of story lines. If *Tamara* has a dozen rooms or stages, then spectators can choose to follow up to 479,001,600 different story lines.[23] Depending upon what story lines they follow, members of the audience shape both their points of view and their knowledge of the larger story.[24] Thus, storytellers (the actors) and story-listeners (the audience) are "co-constructors of each story."[25]

Organizational theorist David M. Boje uses "five choice points," to illustrate the kinds of choices *Tamara* spectators make as they participate in the play's story:

- Which performing characters will you follow as they make an exit from one room to enter some other room?
- Will you follow a character or wait to see who shows up in one or several rooms?
- Will you follow the same character from one room to the next, or jump to a different character as each exits to different rooms?
- If you came with friend(s), will you split up and follow different characters as they make their exit?
- How will you respond when an actor asks you a question or directs you to move here or there on the stage (you become both spectator and actor, or spectator)?[26]

These questions, though designed for a theater production, stir intriguing ideas for congregational life. For example, what might happen if questions like these were posed to congregations? In what ways might *Tamara* serve as a useful metaphor for congregational life?

Congregations are somewhat *Tamara*-like because they are, in a sense, houses with many rooms. Multiple story lines are enacted simultaneously in a congregation's narrative, and no pastoral leader or congregant has access to all of the story lines. Thus, meaning making depends largely on the stories and interpretations people live out and choose to pursue. Meaning making also depends on congregants' willingness to become subjects or active, self-aware participants in their own stories and the stories of others.

For pastoral leaders, becoming personally aware and encouraging congregants to be awrare of the *Tamara*-like qualities of communal life is complex work. Both pastoral leaders and congregations often craft artfully edited stories about themselves. To maintain these versions of their stories, congregations may cultivate some story lines while ignoring or silencing others. Sometimes congregants may also become unhealthily involved in one another's stories. To become more aware is to deconstruct unhealthy stories and storytelling practices and collaborate to live and tell healthier stories.

In reality, congregations do not embody one story line. Congregations are instead "a multiplicity, a plurality of stories and story interpretations in struggle with one another."[27] Also, whether they realize it or not, people in congregations and neighborhoods share one another's stories. Human lives and stories are interconnected. Thus, to move toward congregational health requires a commitment on the part of pastoral leaders and congregants to getting involved in hospitable ways in both the congregation's and the neighborhood's stories.

Along with the Gospel of John, ministry as formation reminds us: In God's house are many dwelling places (from John 14:2). Congregational health and wholeness comes as people anointed by God's creative Spirit make room for the gospel story to unfold in the diverse story lines of people created in the image and sound of God.

CHAPTER 5

I Love to Tell
the Story

Ministry as Formation and Pastoral Leadership

> *With many such parables [Jesus] spoke the word to them, as they*
> *were able to hear it; he did not speak to them except in parables.*
> *(Mark 4:33-34)*

J esus was a storyteller. A parable teller. Coins, mustard seeds, and
weeds—the "stuff" of everyday life—animated Jesus' stories. Farming,
housecleaning, and bread baking—the actions of everyday life—held
unexpected meanings in Jesus' stories.

Jesus was also a story-listener. The Gospel of Mark illustrates this:
"Now there was a woman who had been suffering from hemorrhages for
twelve years" (Mark 5:25). With these words, the Gospel storyteller
embarks on a narrative that leads to healing and hope.

Mark's fast-paced, action-focused storytelling engages readers' imaginations in Mark 5. Voice topples on top of voice as Jesus climbs out of a boat
and walks along this story's dusty street, and as he makes his way through
the crowd, a woman who has been fighting illness for a dozen years
catches Jesus' attention. She touches the hem of Jesus' cloak. Jesus feels
her touch and stops his journey.

Mark's version of this healing story underscores a message about the
value of hospitable and generous listening. On a dusty street, in the midst
of chaotic crowd clamor, a hurting woman "told him [Jesus] the whole

truth"(Mark 5:33c). The Gospel does not give details of her "whole truth." But we are told that Jesus listened. On his way to the home of Jairus, a powerful religious leader, Jesus stopped and listened to a woman whose name the story does not even offer. After listening to her, Jesus responds: "'Daughter, your faith has made you well; go in peace, and be healed of your disease'" (Mark 5:34).

God calls pastoral leaders to follow Jesus' model. Storytelling and story-listening are essential to effective ministry as formation. While chapter 4 offered prompts for congregational formation, this chapter focuses on two dimensions of pastoral leadership formation:

1. Theological curiosity
2. Story fluency

Theological Curiosity

Through stories, congregations communicate beliefs and values. *Theological curiosity* fosters hospitable story-listening and full-bodied storytelling.

What Is Curiosity?

The New Webster's Encyclopedia of Dictionaries provides a basic definition of the word *curious*. When a person is curious, she has "a desire or inclination to learn something new."[1] To cultivate curiosity, by this definition, is to cultivate a desire for learning.

Robert, Mountain View Church's pastoral leader, recently visited the church cemetery. An illustration of curiosity materialized there amid the granite markers. A young child was walking with her father through the maze of memorials. Peering at the gravestones, the child asked, not once, but three times: "But how do the people get in there?"

The child was curious. She had a desire to learn about something unfamiliar to her. Paying theological attention to this event increased Robert's awareness that this child's momentary curiosity about cemeteries, life, and death opened for her the door to a lifelong journey of learning, a journey likely to evolve and deepen as she grows older. The anecdote has broader application. Curiosity is important to human emotional and spiritual growth.

Educator David Beswick excavated past usages of "curiosity" to unearth historical meanings of the word. His discoveries embellish common understandings and point to some of the ways that curiosity nurtures growth.

Historically, Beswick writes, curiosity referred not only to a desire to learn something new but also to an ability to pay attention to "any object in general or learning a task or to a craft."[2] Thus, "something might have been described as 'curiously wrought,' meaning it was crafted with great care. In the same broader sense of careful attention, curiosity formerly had a sense of being defined as a scientific or artistic interest."[3] To be curious was either to pay scientific or artistic attention or to craft something with care or both.

One other definition of "curiosity" also merits notice. "Curiosity" is a desire for knowledge, but it is also an "inquisitive interest in things which are not of proper concern; nosiness."[4] Both definitions have a bearing on *theological* curiosity and ministry as formation.

What Is Theological Curiosity?

Given the above definitions of "curiosity," what is *theological* curiosity? Faith rests in a degree of assurance or conviction of belief about God. Faith also rests in a degree of assent to those things about God that remain veiled in mystery. Theological curiosity, or the desire to know and understand more about both faith's assurances and mysteries, can stimulate spiritual growth. One reason religion endures, for example, is because people have been and are inquisitive about life's beginnings and purposes.

Words like *wonder* or *awe* expand our vocabulary for theological curiosity. Political philosopher James V. Schall, for example, points to a connection between the English phrases "to be curious" and "to wonder." Both, Schall explains, refer to an innate human desire to understand how life works.[5] This innate desire for understanding sparks curiosity.

Environmentalist Rachel Carson considers "wonder" from another perspective: "If I had influence with the good fairy who is supposed to preside over the christening of all children I should ask that her gift to each child in the world be a sense of wonder so indestructible that it would last throughout life, as an unfailing antidote against the boredom and disenchantment of later years, the sterile preoccupation with things that are artificial, the alienation from the sources of our strength."[6] Carson describes wonder as vital to life. Indestructible wonder, Carson emphasizes, is a source of human strength.

Wonder is also an important dimension of theological curiosity. Again, a dictionary definition is useful. "Wonder," as a noun, is "a feeling of surprise mingled with admiration, caused by something beautiful, unexpected, unfamiliar or inexplicable."[7] The verb, "to wonder," means "to desire or be curious to know something" or "to feel admiration and amazement."[8] Wonder invites us to look at the world and recognize how much we have yet to learn.

Wonder, seasoned with awe, for example, refuses to let us become anesthetized to injustice. "Awe" is "a feeling of reverential respect mixed with fear or wonder."[9] Through wonder's eyes, we see familiar and unfamiliar people, places, and ideas in a new light. Wonder jolts human senses and alters perspectives.

Wonder also cultivates healthy curiosity about life, the world, and God. We foster wonder by fostering an inquisitive nature, by learning how to ask questions. Such questions lead, as we shall see in a moment, to the core of ministry as formation, the arts of storytelling and story-listening.

The "Curious" Identity of Pastoral Leaders

Rabbi Abraham Joshua Heschel was a twentieth-century prophet and Jewish mystic. Horrific world realities such as Hitler's leadership of Germany and more than one world-impacting, life-destroying war punctuated Heschel's life. Yet, Heschel wrote with both a poet's and prophet's voice about wonder and awe: "Awe is an intuition for the dignity of all things.... It enables us to perceive in the world the intimations of the divine.... What we cannot comprehend by analysis, we become aware of in awe."[10] For Heschel, wonder and awe lead to holy deeds.

Beswick probes the dimension of curiosity connected to holy deeds. The word *curiosity* originated with the "English word 'cure,' meaning care."[11] This particular sense of "cure," Beswick points out, now lies fallow in a seldom-used and perhaps even less understood phrase, "the cure of souls," meaning the "care of people." Several Christian traditions, such as the Church of England, continue to use a related word, "curate," to designate priests. A curate, or minister, is responsible for the cure, or care, of souls.

Considered from this historical perspective, theological curiosity is rooted in and grows out of relationships of care, and pastoral leaders are called to model theological curiosity, the care of souls. How do pastoral leaders undertake this task? They model theological curiosity when they embody and proclaim God's story in Christ in their lives. They also embody theological curiosity when they pay attention to others' stories. This requires asking good questions.

"You Have to Ask Questions"

Charles Schulz's philosopher, Linus, contributes to an understanding of theological curiosity. In his work on curiosity, Schall exemplifies this by recounting an amusing *Peanuts* comic strip scene. In this scene, Lucy's self-absorption outrages Linus, and he reprimands her. "You never ask me what I think about something, or what I believe, or what I know, or where I'm going, or where I've been, or anything!" Linus finally walks away vocalizing his frustration: "If you're going to show interest in other people, you have to ask questions."[12]

Linus is right. Asking good questions is a key to effective leadership. Corporate trainer Dorothy Leeds focuses on the leadership "power of questions." Responding to a situation with "What should I say?" maintains Leeds, is quite different than responding with "What should I ask?"[13] Questions kindle dialogue and signal a willingness to listen. They also point to a collaborative leadership style.

A too common corporate mentality, continues Leeds, is a "lecture mentality."[14] When leaders lead out of a lecture mentality, employees grow accustomed to being told what to do rather than being asked what they think. Leaders who lead by asking good questions shift from a lecture mentality to a story mentality. Questions encourage storytelling, and storytelling opens doors to creativity and transformation. Storytelling taps into the depth and breadth of an organization's or community's wisdom.

The following are keys to asking questions that spark substantive, revealing storytelling:

1. Good listening is a key to asking good questions.

   - Quiet the chatter in your head and heart.
   - Be a nonanxious presence.
   - Set aside your own agenda.
   - Listen to the other person and not for yourself in what the other person says.

2. Good diagnostic work is a key to asking good questions.

- Ask yourself, "What does this person need from me right now?"
- What can I ask this person that will encourage her to move toward the next question in her journey?
- What other questions or stories or both lie beneath or behind what I hear this person telling me?

3. Letting curiosity guide your presence with people is a key to asking good questions.

- You cannot control the answers *and* ask good questions at the same time. Do not assume you have the only or best answer for another person. *Make space for others to answer questions.*
- Believe that others incarnate substantive theological wisdom for and responses to life's questions.
- Listen generously.
- Ask open-ended questions that lead to other questions.

4. Paying attention to others is a key to asking good questions.

- Ask questions *to* the personality of the other person instead of *out of* your personality. For example, visual learners may need you to ask specific kinds of questions: "What picture comes to mind when I say that?" Or to get at how a "thinking" person feels, you may need to ask a thinking question: "What does that situation make you think?"

The second definition of "curiosity" cited above bears consideration at this point. *Healthy* theological curiosity is an important aim of pastoral leadership. Gossip or heavy-handed pressures to respond do not arise out of *healthy* theological curiosity. Asking *good* questions leads to freely shared as well as robust congregational storytelling. The following are examples of "good" congregational questions:

- What is your favorite story about this congregation?
- Who are the heroes in the story? Who are the villains?

- What biblical stories come to mind when you think about this congregation?
- What story do you imagine this congregation living out ten years from now?

Storytelling and story-listening questions like these generate theological reflection.

As discussed in chapter 3, theological reflection is vital to congregational health and growth. Theologians Patricia O'Connell Killen and John de Beer write that "theological reflection puts our experience into a genuine conversation with our religious heritage.... It helps us access the Christian tradition as a reliable source of guidance as we search to discover the meaning of what God is doing now in our individual and corporate lives.... Further, it trains us to discern the presence of God's spirit in the social events and movements of our time."[15] Stories generated by theological curiosity provide the substance of reflection. Such reflection accesses experience, Christian tradition, and congregational context as sources for ministry as formation.

Congregations like Mountain View or Southside Avenue, for example, have rich histories. But they need to imagine and move toward new stories. Theological reflection allows congregations to value their pasts while imagining and embodying new stories for the future.

Again, a key to effective leadership in this process is learning to ask good questions. A second, related key occurs as stories emerge, and as pastoral leaders also have to develop *story fluency*.

Story Fluency

Pastoral leaders encourage congregations to explore their identities. Homiletician Lenora Tubbs Tisdale offers some guidelines for this exploratory work. Pastoral leaders, Tisdale observes, are ethnographers: "Donning the hat of ethnographer is not so much about taking on new responsibilities as it is about engaging in everyday ministry with new questions, new perspectives, and new tools for interpretation."[16] Ethnographers become participant-observers in a community and work to understand that community's vision, perspectives, and values.[17]

Pastoral ethnographers discover in congregational storytelling abundant material for identity exploration. In fact, congregational stories are "artifacts" laden with "espoused values" and "tacit assumptions."[18] Theological curiosity unearths these values and assumptions.

Tisdale offers examples of ethnographic congregational questions:

- "Are there any recurring images or metaphors in the congregational story as people tell it that give you insight into how they perceive themselves and their world?"[19]
- "Where are the silences in the storytelling of the congregation—the things everyone knows (or at least all the insiders), but no one talks about?"[20]
- "If you were to plot the story of this congregation, like the plot of a novel, what would that plotline look like?"[21]

Wrestling with questions like these leads to story fluency.

What is story fluency? To be "fluent" is "to be capable of moving with ease."[22] Effective ministry as formation requires what educator Marina Bers calls "narrative fluency." To achieve narrative fluency means "becoming familiar with the narrative genre, and in particular, with the relationship between storytelling and identity formation."[23] To achieve narrative fluency, or story fluency, is to learn to tell one's story with integrity, self-awareness, and skill.[24] To achieve narrative fluency is also to move with some ease between storytelling, story-listening, and identity formation.

Healthy theological curiosity is a gift pastoral leaders can offer congregations. Story fluency is also a gift, a gift pastoral leaders can offer their congregations and themselves. In fact, a pastoral leader's story fluency *begins* with healthy self-reflection and self-awareness. As pastoral leaders become more fluent in telling their own stories with depth and authenticity, they can more effectively facilitate storytelling and story-listening in their congregations.

Dominant Stories

What is a "dominant story"? The term *dominant story* is linked to narrative therapy. Narrative therapist Alice Morgan explains. People's lives, she writes, are multistoried: "There are many stories occurring at the same time and different stories can be told about the same events. No single story can be free of ambiguity or contradiction and no single story can encapsulate or handle all the contingencies of life."[25] But sometimes, as discussed in chapter 4, one story line figures more prominently than others.

Positive outcomes follow from this. For example, emboldened by larger-than-life chronicles of heroism or altruism, people may set aside personal or communal story lines of fear to embody story lines of courage. Jesus' story illustrates this. Characterized by hospitality and inclusivity, Jesus' story motivates pastoral leaders and congregations to live out stories of justice making on behalf of others.

But some dominant stories limit or even sabotage lives and relationships. For example, stories of addiction or violence can saturate people's lives, leaving no room for other stories, or a person can so take on an expected or culturally approved story line that she fails to develop other aspects of her identity; or one cultural group's story can so define a political system or economy that other groups are pushed to the margins. Some stories fuel toxic relationships.[26]

In light of this, ministry as pastoral formation challenges pastoral leaders

- to be more aware of story lines that govern their lives;
- to bolster healthy stories;
- to confront toxic congregational and cultural stories with God's story;
- to hear their stories within God's story; and
- to embrace God's story in Christ as their own.

To summarize, dominant stories, both life-giving and toxic, emblazon people's lives with their colors. Sometimes these stories are so robust they obscure other stories and interpretations of stories. Or they mask alternative ways of "story-ing" life events.[27] Ministry as formation opens up "narrative space" for unexplored or new stories.

Reshaping Our Stories

What is narrative space and how does ministry as formation open up this space? As discussed above, ministry as formation is cultivated as people pay attention to what stories govern their lives. But paying attention is complex work.

The sheer number of stories that compete for a pastoral leader's attention and devotion can be overwhelming. Some of the following "headline stories" might be thought of as stories that grab familial headlines or cultural approval, thus influencing our vocational commitments and focus. Others of the following may live somewhere in pastoral leaders' backgrounds, shaping the way they understand themselves, God, others, and the world around them.

- The Story of the Successful Corporate Executive
- The Story of Being Unsuccessful at Trying New Things
- The Story of the Cancer Survivor
- The Story of the First Child to Graduate from College
- The Story of the Firstborn Daughter
- The Story of the Dysfunctional Family
- The Story of the Politically Active Family

Human lives are a conglomeration of these and other headliner stories, and such stories can exert a significant influence on career choices, decision making, relationships, and faith commitments. In fact, as Morgan suggests, one or more of these headlines may live as titles or subtitles of human life stories.

This is the profound and somewhat mysterious power of stories. Some stories secure our devotion by securing the devotion and attention of family, friends, or colleagues. Choosing to live out such stories may garner family respect or lead to job advancement. Other stories are timid, peeking out of our lives only when we think no one is looking. Consider, for example, the young father who secretly wishes he had attended art school but instead took an administrative job in order to support a wife and new family. The "story of the emerging corporate executive" headlines his life; the "story of the artist who might have been" lies fallow in his soul.

Important to recognize is the extent to which *both* stories color this father's worldview, faith perspective, relationship dynamics, and decision-making. When he looks at his children, for example, he looks at them with a determination that they will have more freedom in their career choices than he had. This determination affects how he parents his children, the opportunities he works to make available to them, and the way he thinks about their futures.

Sometimes the powerful stories that headline human lives nurture positive outcomes, both for the individuals who live them and the communities of which they are a part. In other cases, dominant stories are less healthy, overshadowing life-giving ideas or identities. And, in reality, life stories are even more complex than these two rather dualistic choices imply. Not all people who dream of becoming artists, for example, have the ability to make a living embodying that dream. Life stories are complicated, sometimes difficult to sort out, and often maddeningly illusive and elusive. That is why self-awareness and self-reflection are vital to healthy pastoral leadership.

Again, Robert and Mountain View Church provide an example. Sometimes dominant stories meet head-on with equally powerful but contradictory stories. Robert is experiencing this at Mountain View Church in relation to his preaching. Mountain View Church's seemingly silent response to Robert's sermons has been difficult for him.

Since adolescence, Robert has lived the story of being a good public speaker. This story line is important to his self-understanding and confidence. It undergirds his sense of self-worth and value as a preacher. Dominant stories can do that. They can affirm what we believe about ourselves. But dominant stories can also hide story lines and characters that carry truths important to transformation and growth.

Robert *is* a good preacher. Support garnered in adolescence empowered his voice, and study and practice continue to sharpen his skills as a gospel proclaimer. Until he arrived at Mountain View, Robert always received accolades in response to his preaching. The accolades seasoned and solidified his headline story of being a good public speaker.

Mountain View Church, however, provides little of this familiar kind of support for this headline story because Mountain View members offer little vocal affirmation of Robert's preaching. Robert experiences Mountain View's nonvocal responses to his sermons as a challenge to his dominant story and, thus, to pastoral identity. As painful as this is for Robert, the challenge may contain seeds of healthy personal and, thus, leadership formation.

Questions like the following may help Robert to listen more reflectively to his story as pastoral leader:

- What are some biblical stories of "good" gospel proclaimers? How is "good" preaching defined in those stories?
- Where in the biblical story is silence linked to proclamation?
- Is Mountain View Church's silence a response to Robert's pastoral identity or is it linked to the church's past story of ministry with persons who experienced hearing loss? What other aspects of Mountain View Church's story may explain their tendency toward silence?

- What life stories *other than* the story of being a good public speaker stir feelings of joy or confidence for Robert?
- How can these stories become more lively parts of Robert's pastoral identity?

Asking questions like these opens up narrative space in Robert's life as a person of faith and pastoral leader.

Ideally, congregations and pastoral leaders do formative work together. Therefore, Mountain View Church, too, has a responsibility to engage in reflection. For Mountain View Church, this might mean communal theological reflection on the congregation's and Robert's shared stories:

- What voices accompany the "face of God" in this place?
- Where in the biblical story do we find nonvocal "sounding places" that nevertheless give voice to God's truths?
- What congregational stories do we want to hear more often or give more energy to?

Robert cannot hear Mountain View's responses to his ministry. Ironically, the congregation's past story is about empowering people with hearing impairments to hear in a different way.

- What new story might emerge where Robert's story and the congregation's story intersect?
- What biblical story might energize a new communal story?

Moving toward Transformation

Multiple stories govern human life and relationships. Along with religious stories, political, cultural, and global stories also shape beliefs, commitments, and worldviews. For example, Ben is a Mountain View Church elder. He remembers in detail April 4, 1968, the day Martin Luther King Jr. was assassinated. Ben was fifteen years old. His best friend was an African American schoolmate and neighbor. The story changed Ben's and his friend's lives.

Gerald and Maude are founding members of Mountain View Church. A different story lives large in their lives. Their grandson is an Army lieutenant stationed in Baghdad. Reports of bombs exploding in Baghdad are more than CNN sound bites on Gerald's and Maude's soundscape.

Mountain View Church members live in a world battered by globe-altering events. But immersion in story teaches us. Each congregation contributes unique wisdom to what the world knows about God. Congregations carry this wisdom in their souls *as congregations* even though their actions do not always reflect it and they are not always aware of it.[28] A key to healthy ministries is *re-formation* of a congregation's tacit wisdom into more explicit knowledge that can be utilized to share God's story *in that place and time*. Pastoral leaders are charged with facilitating formative processes that lead to this kind of re-formation.

Cautionary Tales

Storytelling and story-listening can be life-giving ministerial practices. But to be healthy, both require clarity about boundaries and a keen sense of pastoral authority and professional ethics.

Pastoral Authority

Several questions about pastoral authority perplex Robert. Two of them are:

- What is my authority as one called to incarnate the story of a pastoral leader?
- How do people in the congregation view my pastoral authority?

Multiple definitions of ministerial authority dot congregational landscapes.[29] Contemporary culture also touts numerous understandings of authority. Thus, the terrain of ministerial authority can be treacherous and confusing.

Putting storytelling and story-listening at the center of ministry as formation encourages a certain type of ministerial authority. In fact, as we have seen, storytelling and story-listening invite congregations and pastors to share authority.

But leaders sometimes become entangled in seemingly contradictory kinds of ministerial authority. For example, what might be termed "priestly authority" may be called for at a dying church member's bedside. But managerial authority is expected at the conference room table.

Storytelling and story-listening and the authority associated with them can function healthfully in both settings. But the authority that fuels storytelling and story-listening may be unfamiliar to pastoral leaders and congregants. Life *among* the people animates narrative ministerial authority. Narrative ministerial authority is authority *with* others. Cultivating this kind of authority sometimes requires pastoral persistence and patience.

Why deem this a cautionary tale? Pastoral leaders who embrace narrative ministerial authority take on a responsibility to pay attention to *all* voices. This requires pastoral sensitivity. It also requires prophetic boldness to make space for neglected or rejected voices. Balancing these responsibilities can be risky and energy-draining work.

Even so, pastoral leaders are charged with being consistent in their attitudes and approaches to relationships and decision making. In fact, consistency in leadership is a key to congregational health. This is why pastoral leaders sometimes need mentoring or coaching relationships to help them develop healthy practices of self-reflection. Such practices are vital to sustaining consistent, balanced relationships with congregations.

Shared authority that emerges from storytelling and story-listening requires pastoral self-awareness, spiritual health, and inner confidence. Weary or embattled pastors sometimes lack all three. Pastoral self-care is essential.

Storytelling and Story-Listening Power Dynamics

Not all stories are beneficial, and not all storytellers are healthy. Discerning story health or toxicity is a complex, risky business. Several cautions are in order:

- Pastoral leaders who encourage storytelling vulnerability have a responsibility to be competent, trustworthy listeners.
- Not all storytelling should be or can be public. Pastoral leaders have a responsibility to shape appropriate and safe personal and congregational storytelling parameters.
- Healthy professional boundaries are essential. Congregants sometimes share personal stories with pastoral leaders in times of emotional or spiritual crisis. Pastoral leaders have a responsibility to be aware of and respect power dynamics in storytelling and story-listening.

• Stories sometimes reveal needs that require other than pastoral expertise. Pastoral leaders have a responsibility to discern when to refer people to other professionals.

Concluding Thoughts

Congregational health and pastoral health are linked. Pastoral leaders sometimes become so immersed in ministerial responsibilities and tasks that they lose sight of who they are *as individual persons of faith,* or they grow tired from organizational struggles, or personal crises take a toll. Healthy ministry emerges when pastoral leaders learn to listen continually for God's story within their own stories. God's story energizes and renews. God's story also fuels healthy and holistic ministry as formation.

PART 3

Ministry as Transformation

CHAPTER 6

Transforming Congregations

We turn again to the Gospel of Luke. Luke 4 narrates the story. Jesus stands to read in worship. A synagogue leader hands him a sacred scroll. Reading from the scroll, Jesus gives voice to the prophet Isaiah's clarion call.

To synagogue listeners that day, the words must have sounded familiar, yet unfamiliar. Spoken aloud by Jesus in worship, Isaiah's ancient words took on new life:

> "The Spirit of the Lord is upon me,
>   because [the Lord] has anointed me
>   to bring good news to the poor.
> [The Lord] has sent me to proclaim release to the captives
>   and recovery of sight to the blind,
>   to let the oppressed go free,
> to proclaim the year of the Lord's favor." (Luke 4:18-19)

God invites Christian congregations of every age to take up Isaiah's and Luke's prophetic threads and, following Jesus' model in Luke 4, weave "the year of the Lord's favor" anew.

Two questions animate this call:

1. How can congregations take up God's weaving work in and for today's world?

2. What textures and hues do today's congregational voices and identities contribute to the gospel tapestry?

Ministry as transformation can be thought of as the loom on which these questions are woven.

In weaving, one set of threads is stretched across a loom and held taut throughout the creation of the fabric. These taut threads are called the *warp* threads. A second set of threads, called the *weft*, is woven in and out of the warp.[1]

Four threads can be considered ministry as transformation's *warp* threads:

1. transformation;
2. just values;
3. responsibility and possibility; and
4. imaginative questions.

Theological educator Ola I. Harrison composed a hymn in 1988 that used weaving as a metaphor for God's work. The hymn celebrates God's call to all people to take up the world transforming work of weaving "threads of justice and shalom."[2] This chapter explores that call as central to ministry as transformation. Three of the above warp threads—"transformation," "just values," and "responsibility and possibility"—are this chapter's focus. A fourth thread, "imaginative questions," is the subject of chapter 7.

Weaving: A Metaphor for Ministry as Transformation

Homiletician Christine M. Smith crafts lively words about the centuries-old art of weaving: "The image of weaving is expansive and visionary, suggesting ways the world might be seen, the Christian faith proclaimed, the faithful life lived. It is an image that has limitless ways of affirming and proclaiming wholeness and integration in the life of faith. Weaving ultimately points to justice in the world because this image has at its heart the interlacing of conflict and struggle with vision and hope. I choose weaving … because weaving is a strong, powerful image that ultimately embodies the wholeness it suggests."[3] Smith uses weaving as a metaphor for Christian proclamation. Following Smith's lead, one can also use weaving as a metaphor for ministry as transformation:

- A weaving metaphor unites form and function in ministry.
- A weaving metaphor emphasizes connections and connectedness in ministry.
- A weaving metaphor honors ancient traditions while encouraging innovation in ministry.

A weaving metaphor unites form and function in ministry. Much like potters, weavers see multiple possibilities in organic materials. Using multi-hued, multitextured threads, weavers create fabrics of beauty and purpose, form and function. Weavers are also skilled technicians. Weaving threads into whole pieces of cloth demands both technical skill and an instinctive sense of design.

Ministry as transformation also demands technical skills and a sense of gospel design. Pastoral leaders and congregations, as we saw in chapter 3, are called to unite form and function in life and faith. A weaving metaphor encourages pastoral leaders and congregations to seek balance between creative theological ideas and day-to-day congregational practicalities.

A weaving metaphor emphasizes connections and connectedness in ministry. A weaving metaphor for preaching, Smith writes, calls the preacher "to see [his or her] own unique life tapestry as fundamentally and intimately related and interwoven with the tapestries of all others."[4] Neither pastoral leaders nor congregations can afford to see themselves and their ministries as isolated from the world. Such a view is unrealistic. God calls pastoral leaders and congregations to take contrasting life strands and fashion them into cohesive theological designs and patterns that make a difference in the world. In order to respond faithfully to this call, congregations must cultivate healthy connections within their communities and with the world around them.[5]

A weaving metaphor honors ancient traditions while encouraging innovation in ministry. Weavers today are keepers of ancient weaving wisdom, often weaving into new designs and patterns wisdom passed down from previous generations of weavers. Again, Smith links these characteristics of weaving to preaching: "The craft of weaving always involves the process of uniting and integrating separate strands into an interwoven whole. Sometimes the weaving depicts real-life situations and experiences in a very explicit way within the weaving itself, while at other times the very interwoven nature of the weaving portrays a vision of unity and wholeness. There are countless methods, styles, and types of weaving, but the essence of the craft is that it always involves the process of uniting and integrating separate strands into an interwoven whole."[6] This integrative, justice-making work toward wholeness is also the work of ministry as transformation. Healthy congregations value and learn from their histories and weave parts of those histories into present and future ministry designs.

Congregations are called to bring good news to the poor, proclaim release to the captives, and let the oppressed go free. This is weaving work. This is transforming work. We turn now to explore the first of the four strands on the ministry as transformation loom: *transformation*.

Transformation

> The spirit of the Lord GOD is upon me,
>   because the LORD has anointed me;
> he has sent me to bring good news to the oppressed,
>   to bind up the brokenhearted,
> to proclaim liberty to the captives,
>   and release to the prisoners;
> to proclaim the year of the LORD's favor. (Isaiah 61:1-2a)

After reading aloud a text from Isaiah 61, Broadview Church's pastoral leader, Tom, announced from the pulpit: "The core of prophetic consciousness is feeling pain." On a rare Sunday away from the pulpit at Southside Avenue Church, Andrea worshiped at Broadview Church during a weekend visit with her parents. Tom's sermon was prophetic for her as a pastoral leader and person of faith.

Broadview Church, a midsized congregation, stands at suburb's edge in a large southern city. Many of Broadview's middle- to upper-middle-class members battle on the frontlines of social causes. These social causes season Sunday worship announcements. For example, Sheila broadcasts news about a statewide green energy program. Ed announces a citywide literacy drive. Claire uses the church bulletin to recruit volunteers for a local nonprofit ministry agency.

Tom developed a sermon series to educate his socially conscious congregation about Hebrew prophets and the prophetic tradition. He wanted congregants to be more aware of connections between their social convictions and faith traditions. The first sermon in the series shed light on threads of Isaiah's prophecies that reappear in Luke's Gospel.

In the sermon, Tom asked the same question that theologian Howard Thurman asked in the 1940s: What do "the teachings and life of Jesus have to say to those who stand, at a moment in human history, with their backs against the wall" ?[7] To explore biblical prophetic writings today, and perhaps in any age, is to be challenged by Thurman's question. The question stood at the heart of Tom's sermon. For ministry as transformation to be effective, Christian congregations need to embody the prophetic consciousness depicted in Hebrew Scriptures.

Prophetic Consciousness and Transformation

Isaiah and Jesus both announce God's reign. Another look at Jesus' vocalization of Isaiah 61 in Luke illumines this:

> "The Spirit of the Lord is upon me,
>   because [the Lord] has anointed me
>   to bring good news to the poor.
> [The Lord] has sent me to proclaim release to the captives
>   and recovery of sight to the blind,
>   to let the oppressed go free,
> to proclaim the year of the Lord's favor." (Luke 4:18-19)

Jesus' public reading of this text from his religious tradition weaves unexpected colors and designs into Isaiah's vision.

Biblical scholar Jacques Matthey identifies several of these unexpected strands by highlighting differences between Luke 4:18-19 and Isaiah 61:1-3. Luke 4:18-19, Matthey points out, omits Isaiah's phrase, "to heal the brokenhearted." The Gospel writer replaces this phrase with one from Isaiah 58:6, "to let the oppressed go free."[8] Thus, Matthey argues, at least according to Luke's Gospel account, Jesus emphasizes liberation in his synagogue reading of the text.

Later in Luke 4, Matthey continues, the Gospel narrator depicts Jesus retelling a story from 1 Kings:

> "Truly I tell you, no prophet is accepted in the prophet's hometown. But the truth is, there were many widows in Israel in the time of Elijah, when the heaven was shut up three years and six months, and there was a severe famine over all the land; yet Elijah was sent to none of them except to a widow at Zarephath in Sidon." (Luke 4:24-26)

God's promised liberation, Jesus' storytelling suggests here, includes all people, even those outside the community of Israel. Anointed by the Spirit to "bring good news," Jesus, as preacher, reinterprets Isaiah and the prophetic tradition and challenges his contemporaries.

Tom's sermon underscored the immediacy and inclusiveness of Jesus' synagogue announcement: "'Today this scripture has been fulfilled in your hearing'" (Luke 4:21). "The time for God's vision of justice is now," Tom declared, echoing Jesus' voice in Luke. "The time to end oppressive conditions is now."

To illustrate, Tom painted a vivid picture of escalating domestic violence in cities and suburbs and reminded listeners of racial injustices in their own city. He also spoke about global atrocities committed against poor and oppressed persons. "All people need justice and liberation from these and other oppressive situations *now*," Tom insisted. Individual commitments to social justice such as that exhibited by Broadview Church members are important to the gospel cause of justice and liberation. But congregations also need to proclaim and embody God's prophetic word collectively *as God's church.*

Tom's sermon caused Andrea to think about Latino and Latina persons living in the Southside community. What does Jesus' proclamation in Luke 4 mean for struggling immigrants, she wondered as the sermon ended. She also thought about Southside Avenue Church. What do Jesus' proclamations or a prophetic consciousness mean for congregations facing economic difficulties? What patterns of transformation might a prophetic consciousness weave in her congregation and neighborhood?

Jewish theologian Abraham J. Heschel points to *divine pathos* as a primary source of prophetic consciousness: "The fundamental experience of the prophets is a fellowship with the feelings of God . . . a communion with the divine consciousness which comes about through the prophet's reflection of, or participation in, the divine pathos."[9] *Divine pathos* is God's ability to feel sorrow for or to suffer with those who suffer. To use Thurman's language, divine pathos is God's ability to feel with those "whose backs are against the wall."[10] To have a prophetic consciousness, again echoing Heschel, is to have "fellowship with the feelings of God."[11] Thus, to have a prophetic consciousness is to join God in *feeling with* those who suffer. It is to share God's compassion for oppressed persons.

But emotion alone is not sufficient to make ministry transforming. *Divine pathos* is interwoven with *divine ethos*. *Divine ethos* is how God incarnates divine pathos in actions that lead to justice and liberation.

God calls congregations and pastoral leaders to revive pathos-ethos connections in their lives and ministries. This means that God calls congregations and pastoral leaders to *feel with* and thus *stand with* oppressed persons. The converse is also true. God calls congregations to stand with and thus feel with oppressed persons.

Some challenging questions emerge for congregations who want to cultivate a prophetic consciousness:

- Who are the oppressed in our community?
- What are we doing to hear their stories, in other words to feel with and stand with them?
- What does our congregation offer to those whose backs are against the wall?
- What does the gospel offer?
- How are pathos and ethos connected in our congregation's story?
- What changes do we need to make to see our neighbors not as objects of concern but as brothers and sisters?

Isaiah's and Jesus' prophetic tapestries await contributions from today's prophets. God calls congregations and pastoral leaders to imagine God's tapestry anew. God calls congregations to weave their threads of justice making and peace into Isaiah's and Jesus' proclamations announcing the "day of the Lord's favor."

Leading Transformation

Tom's sermon stirred Andrea's prophetic imagination. The sermon also stirred a question that corporate management expert John Kotter asks: How do leaders motivate change? Kotter's book, *Leading Change*, addresses this question. To initiate change in corporations, Kotter argues, leaders have to establish "a sense of urgency."[12]

Leading congregational change shares characteristics with leading corporate change. Pastoral leaders also need to establish a sense of urgency in order to spark congregational change. But a caution is in order. Sometimes needs peripheral to a congregation's *Christian* identity can motivate the sense of urgency. Andrea wrestles with this reality. She believes Southside Avenue Church can make a positive difference in the Southside neighborhood. For her, making such a difference is what ministry is all about and for that reason is work of an urgent nature. But Andrea fears the congregation's urgent desire for change may be tied more closely to financial and membership shortfalls than to gospel mandates and promises.

Several questions essential to ministry as formation surface at this juncture:

- How do pastoral leaders balance prophetic imagination and day-to-day administrative tasks?
- What impact does a prophetic consciousness have on problems such as budget shortfalls?
- What kind of transformation revives congregational programs *and* activates prophetic consciousness?

Responses weave in and out of a second warp thread on the ministry as transformation loom: *just values*.

Just Values

An often heard pastoral lament is woven into much congregational life today: "We changed our administrative structure and our curriculum. We even changed the way we worship. We have made many changes, and I am working harder than ever before. But nothing *really* seems different. We still are not growing. We won't meet our budget again this year. Members don't seem energized, and I'm not energized either. I am tired of managing all of the tasks. I'm just not sure this is what I was called to do."

This lament grows out of a perplexing congregational reality. Structural and programmatic changes alone are not enough to lead to spiritual renewal or health. Spiritual renewal and health require deeper awareness of and commitment to gospel values.

Christian social change advocate Jim Wallis underscores this: "Neither religious nor secular fundamentalism can save us, but a new spiritual revival that ignites deep social conscience could transform our society. Movements do change history, and the strongest ones are those with a spiritual foundation. Most important of all is the spiritual power of hope, which may be the only thing that can finally overcome our too characteristic cynicism."[13] Wallis's statement challenges all congregations, regardless of theological perspective, to reignite the hope that springs from a social, or prophetic, consciousness. To reignite this hope, congregations need to reconnect with biblical prophetic roots. Hope, rooted in prophetic consciousness, is a gospel value that sparks transformation.

Gospel Values and Congregational Change

"To transform" is from the Latin *transformare*, which means "to change in composition or structure" or "to change in character or condition."[14] This dictionary definition incorporates the word *change*. But transformation is about more than change alone. *The Merriam-Webster Online Dictionary's* entry for the verb form of "change" highlights the nuance. "To change" comes from the Latin *cambiare*, "to exchange."[15] In its most literal sense, "to change" is to substitute or exchange one thing for another.

Congregations can manufacture changes when they replace one budget, committee chair, or even pastoral leader with another. Or they can engineer changes when they exchange a new curriculum or worship format for old ones. Changes like these may even be important to congregational health and growth. But threads of *transformation* spring not from these kinds of changes but from congregational values.

The following questions are helpful as congregations seek, and perhaps even reconsider, their values, commitments, and beliefs:

- What values are woven into our congregational tapestry?
- What values are missing from congregational designs and patterns?
- What is the source of our values? What makes our values "gospel" values?
- How do we imagine our future tapestry? What values give texture to that tapestry?

These questions imply a conviction about leading change: *healthy congregational transformation begins with a focus on values.*

Can Just Values Lead to Transformation?

Transformation is not a congregational *goal*. Transformation is an ongoing congregational *process* stimulated by three interrelated questions:

1. Who are we?
2. What do we believe?
3. How does God want us to proclaim what we believe?

These questions shape a values-centered approach to leading congregational transformation.

Several Southside Avenue congregational leaders are skeptical about this approach to change: "We need to confront our problems head-on." Values-centered approaches, they argue, do not speak concretely enough to issues of day-to-day congregational survival. One of the church deacons expressed his perspective succinctly: "To make a commitment to sorting out our values will not put additional money in the offering plate next week. The roof needs to be repaired now." These skeptics raise an important question: *"Are just values enough for congregational survival?"*

Corporate professional Stephen Covey responds: "To the degree people recognize and live in harmony with such basic principles as fairness, equity, justice, integrity, honesty, and trust, they move toward ... survival and stability."[16] Clear principles or values, Covey continues, "constitute the roots of every family and institution that has endured and prospered."[17] Principles based on trust and integrity build relationships of trust and integrity.

Covey's insights are valuable for congregations. Trust-based relationships are sources of healthy congregational ministries because they promote more effective short-term problem solving and more imaginative visions of the future. Trust-based relationships also lead to communal stability.

What makes trust and integrity essential *congregational* characteristics? Trust and integrity are gospel values. Howard Thurman discusses from a theological perspective the connection between gospel values and relationships.

For Thurman, relationships are the beauty and strength of a faith community's tapestry. Relationships are also a source of tremendous risk. Thurman ties the threads of relationships directly to God's grace and justice: "The religion of Jesus makes the love-ethic central.... Once the neighbor is defined, then one's moral obligation is clear.... Every [person] is potentially every other [person's] neighbor. Neighborliness is non-spatial; it is qualitative. A [person] must love his [or her] neighbor directly, clearly, permitting no barriers between."[18] "Just" values, values characterized by trust and integrity, emanate from God's grace and Jesus' love-ethic.

Thus, to emulate God is to love our neighbors directly, "permitting no barriers between." Missions-focused stewardship campaigns are not enough. Social ministries programs alone are not enough. Gospel transformation depends on just values centered in and saturated by Jesus' love-ethic. Such values lead to qualitative, face-to-face relationships.

Can just values generate prophetic consciousness *and* meet congregational survival needs? The question invites another consideration of the assertion at the beginning of this section. Transformation is not a goal or product of congregational life. Likewise, just values are not products. Just values are implicit to a *process* of congregational daily life and growth together in God's grace.

Congregations without doubt face urgent crises that require timely and effective decision making. Southside Avenue Church's budget shortfall exemplifies this. Strategies for day-to-day survival and decision making thus remain a necessary part of congregational life and leadership. But just values are also essential if decision making is to be centered in a gospel love-ethic and lead to congregational well-being and prophetic communal action.

Chapter 4 explored how storytelling approaches recast financial questions. Just values can also recast congregational administrative questions. In fact, just values contribute to short-term and long-term strategies by cultivating ethical, hospitable, and neighborly behaviors in all congregational decision-making processes. In order for just values to be effective, however, congregations must gain clarity about their identities, purposes, and commitments in their particular contexts. They must gain clarity about their gospel responsibilities.

This moves the discussion to a third warp thread on the ministry as transformation loom: *responsibility and possibility.*

Responsibility and Possibility

Congregations are called to weave public patterns of gospel justice and truth.[19] Put another way, congregations hold places of social and even political responsibility in their communities. When they stand with confidence in those places of responsibility, congregations can effectively proclaim gospel possibilities. Thus, we come to the third warp thread on the ministry as transformation loom: *responsibility and possibility.*

By embracing gospel responsibility and possibility, pastoral leaders integrate two seemingly contradictory ministerial functions. On one hand, pastoral leaders must be able to perform their tasks within the structures and demands of institutional life. On the other hand, pastoral leaders must envision possibilities beyond those structures. They must call congregations to their vocations of leadership in the world.

Andrea wrestles with these aspects of ministry as transformation. In her ministry, envisioned prophetic possibilities often clash with congregational administrative responsibilities. For example, Southside Avenue Church members respect Andrea's biblically based social justice convictions. Many of them even agree with Andrea that hospitality toward their neighbors, especially their Latino and Latina neighbors, is a gospel mandate. But budget and membership decline have created a greater sense of congregational urgency than the call to gospel hospitality. Also, ongoing budget and membership crises deplete members' energy and dull their imaginations. Thus, Southside Avenue Church members have a hard time making a connection between diminishing returns in their offering plates and neighborliness toward financially challenged immigrants who live down the street.

In addition, along with the above administrative complexities, when congregations claim public places of responsibility and leadership, a perplexing tangle of other issues is sometimes generated. Current political debates about the status of immigrants or about raising the minimum wage are examples. Sometimes neighborliness draws people into political snarls such as these. Put theologically, sometimes embodying a prophetic consciousness—feeling with and standing with those in need—is risky work and does not lead to popularity or financial success for individuals or numerical success for congregations. Nevertheless, the gospel call publicly to proclaim and embody justice reverberates from the time of Isaiah through Luke's Gospel to congregations today. God calls congregations and their leaders to take their places with courage and conviction at the public loom.

Taking a Place at the Public Loom

Tapestries vital to communal, national, and global health are designed and woven at public looms. God commissions congregations as theologically dissimilar as Southside Avenue and Broadview churches to take up God's threads of justice and grace at these looms. But what does this mean in relationship to everyday congregational management responsibilities? How can congregations be publicly prophetic if they cannot make ends meet?

A resource for response resides in the word *vocation.* *Vocation* derives from a Latin word meaning "summons."[20] A second Latin word associated with vocation, *vox,* means "voice."

Andrea sometimes reflects on her "summons" to ministry. After several years as a corporate executive, she grew restless in her job. Her values and her work too often seemed to pull in opposite directions. She began to sense a restlessness to invest her skills and gifts in a different vocation. Spiritual reflection, conversations with friends, and prayer converged. Andrea experienced a summons, or call, from God to professional ministry.

Other clergypersons also talk about God's call, narrating how God summoned them to do God's work. The one called may not be able logically to explain her call. But she knows that she heard God's voice. Perhaps the divine call echoed in a book. Or maybe God's bidding persisted in a teacher's or minister's encouragement. Or maybe the summons came on a starry night when celestial beings appeared in the heavens and announced the news. After all, this is how God summoned shepherds in Luke's Gospel to Bethlehem to see the Savior of the world.

Whatever the mode of the call, most pastoral leaders recount a sense of being summoned by God to professions of ministry. But people other than pastoral leaders are also called to do God's work. People in other vocations also experience a summons to make a difference while making a living. Southside Avenue Church members narrate many stories of such calls:

- A man works during the week at a print shop and sings bass in a traveling gospel quartet on the weekends.
- A mother of two teenagers coordinates a spiritual direction program for single parents.
- A farmer plants and harvests ten extra acres of corn each year for the local food bank.

Gospel-story fibers like these converge in congregational tapestries large and small. They depict God's presence in the world. They also point to another important meaning of vocation.

To be created in God's image, as we saw in chapter 1, is to be created "in the sound of God." The second Latin word associated with the word *vocation* underscores this. As stated above, the Latin word *vox* means "voice." To have a vocation is to have a voice. Put theologically, vocation has to do with how God expresses God's voice through human voices and stories, *all* human voices and stories. For Southside Avenue Church, embodying this belief may mean becoming more aware that their Latino and Latina neighbors are created in the sound of God.

God calls congregations to bring to public looms Jesus' prophetic announcement: Today, this Scripture is fulfilled in your hearing. Today is the time for change. Today is the time for new colors, textures, and designs.

What does this mean in concrete terms? Ethicist and philosopher William May writes about the public obligation of pastoral leaders and congregations. Just values, he emphasizes, should characterize a congregation's public voice.

Congregations cannot avoid their public responsibilities and remain healthy. An inward focus on individual spiritual growth is only part of a congregation's vocation. Congregations are also called to spin threads of justice and grace out into the world.[21]

May's words challenge congregations to engage more robust processes of public identity exploration: "Some basic elements in the church's understanding of its mission should charge its leaders with wider duties than service to the interior needs of its members and more reliably than occasional, crisis-driven forays into public action."[22] Ministry as transformation is not a programmatic emphasis. Nor is it an occasional or crisis-driven activity. Ministry as transformation is a loom onto which the gospel values and energies of God's people can be woven. When congregations take up the weaving work that is ministry as transformation, gospel justice-making possibilities emerge to challenge and change the world.

Transforming Congregations

Congregational fibers, textures, and threads vary from place to place, and individual congregations are called to identify their unique warp and weft threads. This identifying process is complex work but is an important step toward transformation. Once congregations have begun to name warp and weft threads, they can move with greater clarity toward grace-motivated, justice-making actions.

This chapter calls congregations to transforming work. Howard Thurman's prophetic vision of Jesus underscores the call and extends a challenge:

> For what is human history but [human's] working paper as he [or she] rides high to life caught often in the swirling eddies of tremendous impersonal forces set in motion by vast impulses out of womb of the Eternal. When a solitary individual is able to mingle his [or her] strength with the forces of history and emerge with a name, a character, a personality, it is no ordinary achievement. It is more than the fact that there is a record of his [or her] life—as singular as that fact may be. It means that against the background of anonymity he [or she] has emerged articulate, and particular.[23]

Jesus embodied transforming work. He wove his life threads together with those of his time and place. A personality, a character, and a name emerged. All three endure in congregational identities and actions. Anointed by God's Spirit, congregations can emerge from the tangled mass of human brokenness "articulate" and "particular," weaving communal identities of gospel justice and grace.

CHAPTER 7

Imaginative Questions

She sat on the floor, perched on a cushion in front of a large loom.
As she talked, her hands never stopped moving, weaving in the
different colors of the woof, tamping down the threads, fingering
the next row.
 She barely seemed to glance at the beauty she was creating.
The design was within her. "The rug is all of my experience," she
told me. "It is everything that has ever happened to me, all of my
history."[1]

Designs of transformation live *within* congregations. They reside
with the indwelling Spirit of God and grow out of everything
that has happened to a congregation, all of its history. Designs
of transformation are also enlivened by everything that will ever happen to the congregation in the future. This brings the discussion to the
fourth warp thread on the ministry as transformation loom: *imaginative
questions*.

Imagine, Incarnate, and Lead Transformation

Lyle Schaller is a congregational management consultant. One of his most intriguing books carries a lengthy but telling title, *The Interventionist: A Conceptual Framework and Questions for Parish Consultants, Intentional Interim Ministers, Church Champions, Pastors Considering a New Call, Denominational Executives, the Recently Arrived Pastor, Counselors, and Other Intentional Interventionists in Congregational Life*. In *The Interventionist*, Schaller focuses on the importance to congregational leadership of asking good questions. Schaller asserts that asking substantive questions is at the heart of congregational transformation. Thus, nine of his twelve chapters end with a question.[2]

Congregations who seek health have to learn to thrive faithfully in a world replete with uncertainties and ambiguities. They have to learn to live with organizational complexities that sometimes end with question marks rather than exclamation points. Schaller argues that for pastoral leaders "this often means moving beyond the recommended formula of the 1950s of 'listening and learning.' The new formula ... begins with 'asking questions, asking questions, listening, asking questions, learning, asking questions, listening, and formulating a tentative agenda.'"[3] The most effective way to influence congregational behaviors, Schaller insists, is "to ask questions."[4] To tease out the designs for transformation within congregations, pastoral leaders have to learn to ask imaginative questions.

Again, Southside Avenue Church provides an example. Andrea wants Southside Avenue Church to grow spiritually and organizationally. She imagines a congregational future marked by renewed commitment and confidence. She imagines hearing gospel news heralded meaningfully by her congregation throughout Southside's soundscape. To make these future scenarios realities, Andrea needs concrete guidelines.

In light of her imaginative hopes for the future and her desire for guidelines, the following leadership proposal may surprise Andrea: *A pastoral leader does not need a crystal clear vision of the future. Rather, she needs to know how to articulate questions that encourage her congregation to rediscover its identity.* Embracing a proposal such as this challenges many pastoral leaders' understandings of leadership. Andrea's story illustrates this.

Andrea has a strong desire to demonstrate competence as a pastoral leader. This desire grows out of several dimensions of Andrea's life. Andrea began her vocational journey in the corporate world. Corporate success demands competence, and corporate competence is often defined in terms of competition and power.

At midlife, Andrea made a vocational change from leadership in the corporate world to leadership in the ministry world. Corporate leadership just did not match Andrea's identity or values. But even though Andrea was never motivated by corporate competition or attracted to corporate power, she did strive for excellence in her job.

That vocational characteristic endures. Now, Andrea strives for excellence as a pastoral leader. She wants to excel in her roles as pastoral care provider, administrator, preacher, and teacher. She wants to be a competent, successful pastoral leader.

To be a competent and capable pastoral leader is a healthy goal. What is unhealthy is the notion that being competent means having all of life's or theology's answers. What reinforces this unhealthy notion is the tendency of some congregations to look to pastoral leaders as expert keepers of spiritual and organizational knowledge. In other words, in the minds of some church members and pastoral leaders, competent pastoral leadership is marked not by the ability to *ask* questions but by the ability to *answer* questions.

To go against the grain of these congregational perceptions is taxing work. In fact, embracing a leadership identity of "asker" instead of "answerer" can be a lifelong process of overcoming multiple personal, congregational, and cultural challenges. But learning to ask more often than answer can lead to more effective and healthier pastoral leadership.

How can Andrea and other pastoral leaders embrace identities as pastoral askers? Such a process begins, Schaller suggests, with a leader's awareness of her or his emotional and intellectual "baggage," baggage that takes the form of life assumptions, priorities, and values.[5]

Not surprisingly, given the above assertions, some key questions for pastoral self-reflection assist in cultivating an "asking" identity:

- Am I comfortable asking questions?
- When I do ask questions, what kinds of questions are they? Rhetorical questions? Leading questions? "Yes" or "no" questions? Open-ended questions?
- How often in meetings or in pastoral conversations do I ask questions for which I have preconceived answers?
- What values, life assumptions, or personal priorities fuel these answers?

- Where do I hear my life story in the answers I give and the questions I ask?
- Do I *really* ask questions? In other words, do I ask questions and then let the congregation take ownership of the questions and whatever answers might emerge?

The challenge of embracing an identity as pastoral asker is both a personal and theological challenge. Consider this scenario: If Andrea believes God is incarnate only in her (or more incarnate in her than in church members), then she has to do most (if not all) of the theological and ministerial work. She has to take responsibility for envisioning the future, developing strategies, and implementing plans. In this scenario, congregations function largely as recipients of a pastoral leader's superior knowledge and insight.

An incarnational understanding of ministry as transformation suggests an alternative scenario: If Andrea trusts that all people are created in the image and sound of God, then the work of imagining the future and weaving transformation belongs to the congregation as a whole. In fact, if Andrea believes God is incarnate in the congregation as a whole, then theological questions are generated in and imagined by the congregation as a whole. They are not imposed on the congregation as templates for thought, belief, or action.

In incarnational theologies of ministry as transformation, pastoral leaders invite congregations to share the work of naming God, the world, and themselves in the world. Such an invitation contributes to healthy congregational change. Several congregational questions (not theological answers) provide spiritual fuel for healthy change. The following examples are directed toward Southside Avenue Church. Similar questions, guided by congregational context, can be posed to other congregations:

- Can Southside Avenue Church extend an incarnational theology to its neighborhood?
- Can Southside Avenue Church make space for its Latino and Latina neighbors to name themselves in the Southside neighborhood?
- Can Southside Avenue Church make room for its neighbors to proclaim the gospel in their own voices and stories?

Problem Solving and the Chaos of Change

To echo chapter 6, a perception of urgency about a situation or issue usually precedes congregational change. For Southside Avenue Church, continued budget deficits are the primary source of urgency about needed immediate change. The church's budget committee recently published in the church newsletter a warning that reflects the urgency: "We will not meet our budget this year."

A church member presented Andrea with a solution. "I'd like to contribute enough money to see us through." The budget committee accepted a similar offer from the same church member the previous year. At that time, the committee adopted the strategy as a stopgap measure. "Finances will improve next year," the committee reasoned. But another year has passed, and finances have actually worsened.

Stopgap measures tempt congregations, largely because such measures seem to fend off approaching chaos. They buy time. *But stopgap measures are only temporary solutions and do not often lead to transformation.*

By accepting a generous church member's temporary "fix" the previous year, Southside Avenue Church's budget committee opted for a linear problem-solving approach. Linear problem solving follows a particular trajectory:

- identify the problem;
- outline all possible solutions;
- decide on a solution;
- implement a plan.

Such a problem-solving trajectory is helpful and sometimes necessary, particularly for easily definable problems. When a church's five-year-old air conditioner is broken, for example, a technician can identify the problem, determine solutions, and suggest a repair strategy. A congregational committee can then authorize the repair or choose a different solution.

But congregations do not always face problems as easily resolved as the above air conditioner problem. In fact, today's pastoral leaders and congregations encounter many problems that defy clarity. Operational manager Russell Ackoff makes a statement about corporate managementthat relates to congregational problem solving: "Managers are not confronted with problems that are independent of each other, but with dynamic situations that consist of complex systems of changing problems that interact with each other. I call such situations messes. Problems are abstractions extracted from messes by analysis; they are to messes as atoms are to tables and charts.... Managers do not solve problems; they manage messes."[6]

Ackoff's "messes" do not readily respond to linear problem solving, and congregational problems, sometimes even air conditioner problems, are appropriately labeled "messes."

Southside Avenue Church's budget problems are an example. The budget shortfall requires immediate attention. The church has bills to pay. In that sense, the problem is clearly defined. But at a deeper level, the budget problems are about more than income figures and monetary bottom lines. The budget shortfall is only one issue arising from the messier, more complex issue of congregational identity.

Too often, linear problem solving avoids or ignores larger issues. Short-lived and short-sighted internal changes are sometimes the result. But congregational identity struggles are longer-term problems that do not fit into clearly defined short-term solution packages. Congregational identity struggles are messes. When faced with congregational "messes," pastoral leaders do apply certain professional and administrative skills. More than that, however, pastoral leaders are charged with wading through the messes to find "the right problem to solve."[7]

Alternatives to linear problem solving vary from one congregation to another. Andrea discovered one alternative approach in an unlikely story. Jan, a Southside Avenue Church member, shared her pregnancy story with Andrea.

Jan was forty-three years old when she received the news. "Expect the baby to arrive in September," the doctor announced. Jan and her husband, Dan, had years ago stopped hoping for a child. Her life strategy no longer included a baby. "Once we learned I was pregnant, Dan and I had to let go of what we thought we knew about our lives and even about the world," Jan said, remembering her and her husband's surprise. "Sometimes it is easier to hold onto what you know, even if what you know is limiting. But the unexpected pregnancy taught us that when you let go of what you think you know, you realize how much there is to learn. We had to let go in order to receive the new gift life had for us.

Jan's story was about pregnancy and childbirth. But Andrea recognized the story's broader theological wisdom. Could there be a connection between Jan's story and the congregation's budget story? What problem-solving pattern might emerge if wisdom from Jan's story became a thread in the congregation's approach to its budget difficulties and identity search? What if Jan's story could become a kind of theological and spiritual springboard story?

The following problem-engaging pattern is one possibility:

- Encourage the congregation to let go of what it knows with certainty. Celebrate (or at least accept) the messiness that accompanies letting go.
- Find ways to be creative and innovative *in the midst of* messiness or chaos.
- Accept the possibility, even the probability, that more than one problem is present in this situation and that more than one answer may have value.

Linear problem-solving strategies do eventually emerge from alternative processes like this one. Congregations cannot function without short-term and long-term strategies for a whole assortment of administrative and pastoral tasks. Day-to-day decision making is a necessary part of congregational life and leadership. However, this alternative process challenges congregations to make identity work more of a priority. Or the process at least challenges congregations to connect day-to-day problem solving to identity work. This is important because more effective and enduring responses to congregational problems grow out of healthier identities.

What is the role of pastoral leaders in this process? To move with congregations through chaos to transformation requires pastoral leaders who really trust their congregations with the questions of faith and ministry. It requires pastoral leaders who really believe God is incarnate in their congregations. It also requires leaders who are clear about their own values.

God calls congregations and pastoral leaders to be God's partners. But life's chaos and uncertainty stir fears that have an impact on all congregations. To resist fearful responses in favor of healthier responses involves risk. How do congregations nurture emotional, psychological, and theological hardiness to sustain them as they move through chaos to transformation?

Letting Go of Certainties

Gospel power is not a limited commodity. Political entities, organizations, and institutions perpetuate a myth that power and success are

limited commodities for which people must compete. Corporate consultant Stephen R. Covey resists this myth.

Covey encourages what he calls an "abundance mentality": "The nor-
mal distribution curve, embedded deep in the bowels of both academia
and business, tends to spawn the scarcity mentality because of the per-
ceived 'zero sum' situation.... People with a scarcity mentality tend to see
everything in terms of 'win-lose.' ... People with an abundance mentality employ the negotiation principle of win/win and the communication
principle of seeking first to understand before seeking to be understood.... An abundance mentality springs from an *internal security*, not
from external rankings, comparisons, opinions, possessions, or associa-
tions."[8] An abundance mentality benefits congregations in two dimensions of congregational life: biblical interpretation and theologies of
work. An abundance mentality also cultivates imaginative questions.

Listening to Biblical Voices

"Many voices proclaim God's news in Scripture. The Bible is a tapestry of voices and meanings," Andrea suggested in a recent Sunday school
class. Several people asked for examples.

The requests initiated an important reflection process. Southside
Avenue Church members treasure the Bible as a primary resource for congregational life. However, members' interpretive practices do not always
take advantage of the depth or breadth of biblical wisdom and theology.

If members can learn to listen differently to the Bible, Andrea believes,
they may also be empowered to listen differently to their Latino and
Latina neighbors. The reverse is also true. If members learn to listen to
their Latino and Latina neighbors, they may begin to hear the Bible in
new ways.

Andrea wants to encourage her congregation to let go of (or at least
loosen its hold on) what it knows "with certainty" about the Bible. Some
in the congregation have already let go of one such certainty. More than
one church member previously interpreted certain biblical texts about
women as prohibitions to the ordination of women. Yet Andrea is
ordained, and Southside Avenue Church has embraced her as its primary
gospel proclaimer. In order to accept Andrea as their pastoral leader, some
congregants had to let go of what they thought they knew about God and
Scripture.

Andrea wants church members to open their ears to biblical voices that might spur other kinds of transformation. This involves learning to pose to Scripture substantive interpretive questions. A linear approach will not make Andrea's hope a reality. But if she can collaborate with her congregation to imagine different questions about the Bible, they may together open new theological doors. They may even move closer to opening the church's literal doors into the community.

Andrea plans to use a story-telling and story-listening strategy to reorient her congregation's approach to biblical interpretation. Her teaching plan contains the following components:

- In an initial session, the leader invites each participant to share with a partner a Scripture passage that is meaningful to him or her. Each participant is invited to share a life story that reveals the source of the passage's importance in the participant's life.
- In a second, collaborative, session, the leader asks a volunteer to share with the whole group her or his Scripture text and story. Other participants are encouraged to listen generously through a lens of theological curiosity. Participants are encouraged to reflect on how the volunteer's interpretation invites them to hear the biblical text in new ways.
- In a follow-up session, the leader presents a range of interpretive views on several texts about which participants shared stories. Views can be collected from sources including scholarly interpretations, sermons, poetry, and music. Participants are again encouraged to reflect on how to hear the biblical texts in new ways.

Such an approach to Scripture is grounded in an abundance mentality. Biblical truth is not a limited commodity. Nor is finding or announcing the one absolute truth about any particular biblical passage the responsibility of those who have pastoral authority.

To embrace this perspective stirs questions crucial to congregational identity:

- How are our neighbors' voices and stories part of the gospel's tapestry?
- What do we need to do to welcome these voices into our theologies?

- What do we need to do to welcome these voices into our congregation?
- What can we do to open the doors to shared growth and learning with our neighbors?

An abundance mentality suggests that biblical texts hold many truths and meanings. An abundance mentality also values the multiple stories and insights individuals bring to biblical texts. Such a mentality affects not only practices of reading the Bible but also perceptions of human work and vocation.

Abundant Theologies of Work

Gospel power is not a limited commodity. Nor is the work associated with the gospel a limited commodity. In other words, professional ministers do not have a corner on gospel wisdom or authority. Pastoral work is not the only sacred or spiritual work.

To echo the first two chapters, human beings are created in the image and sound of God. All people are called to do God's work. This call is not necessarily to do work *in addition to* or *instead of* the work required by a career (though that is sometimes the case). Instead, God's call is a call to holistic human living supported by just values proclaimed within and embodied by communities of faith. In other words, the call to do God's work permeates careers. It permeates all of human living. Thus, human work should, on some level, be sacred work.

Theologian Miroslav Volf underscores this. "All human work done in accordance with the will of God," Volf writes, "is cooperation with God in the preservation and transformation of the world."[9] Luke 4 comes to mind again. Human beings are called to cooperate with God in announcing and embodying God's reign of liberating justice and peace. Sunday worship is one venue for this cooperation. But people are also challenged to cooperate with God in their daily work. They are challenged to revive in their daily work the pathos-ethos connection.

Spiritual teacher and author Matthew Fox puts it this way: "Good living and good working go together. Life and livelihood ought not to be separated but to flow from the same source, which is Spirit, for both life and livelihood are about Spirit."[10]

What does this mean? Volf's and Fox's words imply that human work is in some way linked to human spirituality. But the connection is often misunderstood or ignored. From a consumer-oriented perspective, for example, work is what people do for six and sometimes seven days of the week in order to "make a living." Or unemployed and underemployed persons despair at being unable to make a living. Or some people do monetarily noncompensated work such as cooking meals or washing laundry for their families. Or some people do not have the intellectual or emotional resources to acquire and keep jobs that provide a living wage; thus, their work is not always valued or affirmed. Too many workers in our economy, for example, spend forty or more hours per day on their jobs, but still do not have sufficient income to provide adequate meals or dwelling places for their families. In these scenarios, Spirit-infused or Spirit-anointed work is more anomaly than norm. Caution must be exercised, therefore, as we explore the relationship between human work and human spirituality.

Perhaps what is overlooked in the above scenarios and reflections about human work and spirituality is the connection between human work and just values. The Deuteronomist's words challenge us:

> When you reap your harvest in your field and forget a sheaf in the field, you shall not go back to get it; it shall be left for the alien, the orphan, and the widow, so that the LORD your God may bless you in all your rundertakings. (Deuteronomy 24:19)

Work, along with worship, has prophetic and political implications. God's call to action has an impact on human work.

In fact, work and worship are connected. For example, one meaning of the word *liturgy* is "the work of the people." The work of the people in worship is to rehearse language, actions, and values they then strive to embody in daily activities, including their work. Worship cultivates a prophetic consciousness. What are the prophetic and political implications of work and worship? Worship prepares us to participate in what Matthew Fox calls God's "Great Work."[11] The Great Work is God's work of shaping a just and peaceful world.

In the Gospel of Luke, Jesus embodies the Great Work by embodying just values. Individuals and congregations are also called to embody just values in their daily work. Congregations grow healthier and clearer about their identities as they individually and collectively strengthen links between human work, spirituality, and just values. One reason is that individuals begin to resist compartmentalization of livelihood and life, of secular and sacred, in favor of greater everyday holism.

What does this mean for congregations like that of Southside Avenue Church? As Andrea invites congregants to listen in new ways to biblical voices, she might also invite congregants to explore new perceptions of human work and spirituality.

The following questions can guide this work:

- What breathes life into me (as an individual)? Into us (as a congregation)?
- How does my work create good for others? Our work as a congregation?[12]
- How does my work energize me? How does our work as a congregation energize our congregation?
- How does my work empty me?
- Can I describe one of my life's most satisfying experiences?
    - What was I doing?
    - With whom?
    - What was my role (leader, encourager, challenger, and so on)?
    - What skills did I use?
    - What role do I play in my primary work now?
    - What skills do I use?
    - What values are important to me in my work?
    - How do my answers relate to my identity as one called to proclaim?
- How does my work contribute to God's tapestry?
- Where do we hear or see God's wisdom in one another's work? In our congregation's work?

The role of a pastoral leader in such an exercise is important. Not only does the leader encourage and affirm participants, but the leader can also tease out and begin to name shared values present in the stories and insights shared.

A next step for Southside Avenue Church is to weave the above exercise together with work aimed at the congregation's public identity. The following questions might generate important strands for this work:

- What is work like for our neighbors?
- How does our work as individuals and as a congregation create good for our neighbors?
- What is God's Great Work for and with our neighbors?

- How do society's values conflict with our congregation's values? How do society's values limit our neighbors' ability to experience just values in their daily work?

Through human work, God dreams patterns of courage and transformation for all people. New insights and actions emerge as congregations and pastoral leaders say "yes" to ongoing processes of discernment and renewal.

Conclusion

Designs of transformation are within congregations. But they do not reside within programs. Programmatic impulses ebb and flow. What endure are congregational commitments and beliefs. These are weft threads that motivate and sustain transforming work.

Woven into warp threads of transformation, just values, responsibilities and possibilities, and imaginative questions, these weft threads provide vibrancy and strength to congregational fabrics. They also mark patterns and processes of transforming congregational work.

CHAPTER 8

Voice, Clay, and Fiber

Putting It All Together

> The hand of the LORD came upon me, and [the Lord] brought me
> out by the spirit of the LORD and set me down in the middle of a
> valley; it was full of bones. [The LORD] led me all around them;
> there were very many lying in the valley, and they were very dry.
> [The LORD] said to me, "Mortal, can these bones live?" I
> answered, "O Lord GOD you know." Then he said to me,
> "Prophesy to these bones, and say to them: O dry bones, hear the
> word of the LORD. Thus says the Lord GOD to these bones: I will
> cause breath to enter you, and you shall live. I will lay sinews on
> you, and will cause flesh to come upon you, and cover you with
> skin, and put breath in you, and you shall live; and you shall
> know that I am the LORD. (Ezekiel 37:1-6)

"Can these bones live?" God poses the question to Ezekiel, a priest
to sixth-century exiles. Many congregations today experience
both pain and possibility in the centuries-old question. Can God
teach our weary bones to dance again?

Southside Avenue Church's anniversary celebration highlighted
vibrant fibers from the church's past. Now, church members wrestle with
Ezekiel's question as they imagine their next fifty years: "Can our bones
live?" Fabric woven solely from the fibers of the past no longer fit who

this congregation is becoming. What is next for Southside Avenue Church?

As pastoral leader, Andrea wants to encourage Southside Avenue congregants to explore questions about their future from some different perspectives. What vessels can this congregation place on its communion table that will hold life-giving hopes and dreams? Whose voices will Southside Avenue Church welcome to that table? What fabric can the congregation weave to clothe those dreams and voices?

We have engaged questions like these by focusing on three dimensions of ministry—ministry as proclamation, formation, and transformation. *Keep the Call* deems each dimension important as pastoral leaders and congregations seek ministry designs that *really work* for them and their congregations. This chapter explores ways to put the three dimensions together.

It may be helpful at this point to revisit questions that fueled *Keep the Call's* introduction:

- What is the role of congregations in changing communities?
- What types of ministry are most effective as congregations and their leaders seek their identities, values, and purposes in proclaiming the gospel?
- How do congregations interact innovatively and authentically with tradition *and* the world so that God and faith come alive in new ways?
- Where can leaders find resources to cultivate their own deepest callings and passions while serving in communities whose identities are in transition?

Congregations today have access to many innovative resources for responses to these questions. These resources range from program templates to organizational designs to pre-packaged budgeting strategies. Some of these resources provide useful information and ideas. However, some congregations focus too exclusively on external resources or templates for their ministries.

Such a focus can put obstacles on the path to congregational health and growth. The reason? Ministry cannot be conceived as a "one-size-fits-all" template. In fact, cut-and-paste solutions are not realistic for most congregational problems. One reason is that congregations are diverse and wonderfully idiosyncratic. Models or programs that work for one congregation may be minimally successful or even disastrous in another congregation.

Keep the Call also recognizes that congregational *health* may look different in different congregations. So, too, may Spirit-infused and Spirit-anointed ministries. Even ministry *success* may take on different shapes and colors depending on a congregation's values and identity.

Thus, *Keep the Call* does not pose solutions to specific congregational problems. In fact, *Keep the Call* does not view ministry as a program or product or even as a strategy. Instead, *Keep the Call* conceives ministry as a *process*. In this process, each person in a congregation has a creative role. Each person is invited to imagine questions such as "who are we?" and "what are our callings as a congregation?" *Keep the Call* insists that enduring solutions to congregational problems emerge over time as congregations become clearer about their identities and their public vocations.

For Andrea, the focus of *Keep the Call's* leadership process is curled up in a question mark at the end of an important query: What should our congregation do next? Thinking of ministry in three dimensions (proclamation, formation, and transformation) taps into the spiritual wisdom of her congregation. Each dimension carves out space for Southside Avenue Church and its members to grow more fully into their unique Christian identities. But these dimensions do not provide specific steps for expanding the budget or building bridges to the church's Latino and Latina neighbors. These dimensions do not substitute any exclamation points for Andrea's pastoral leadership question mark.

Instead, determining next steps requires of Andrea a stance or perspective required of all healthy pastoral leaders. Andrea is several years into her role as Southside Avenue Church's pastoral leader. She has learned much about Southside Avenue's history, personality, strengths, and shortcomings, and she carries in her head multiple blueprints for effective ministry in this community. Some are linked to Scripture; some to her own sense of prophetic calling; others to what she learned in seminary classrooms. Still other ministry blueprints grow out of the stories and dreams of the congregation's members; or are rooted in the theological wisdom Andrea believes lives in the Southside Avenue neighborhood.

Andrea has also begun to build relationships. She has listened to congregational stories, questions, hopes and dreams. Now is the time for Andrea to focus on her next steps as Southside Avenue's pastoral leader.

Chapter 7 underscored one important characteristic of incarnational next steps: *Pastoral leaders are not required to be the sole answer providers in the face of difficult questions*.

What does this mean for Andrea in her future as Southside Avenue's pastoral leader? For her, putting together voice, clay, and fiber may mean facing one truth, then adopting a stance of faith toward another truth.

The first truth Andrea needs to face, at least in terms of Southside Avenue Church's most visibly pressing problems, may be this: "I don't have an immediate or clear solution to the budget problems that we face." In other words, Andrea may have to let go of any need she has to be the pastoral expert who resolves the budget crisis. She may have to let go of her expectations and assumptions about pastoral success. She may also have to encourage her congregation to let go of some of their assumptions.

The second truth is theological and resides in Andrea's belief in God's grace: "I am *learning how* to do ministry that cultivates hope within this congregation and perhaps even within this neighborhood. This congregation and I *can* make a positive difference." This second, two-part truth is not yet a reality. Both Andrea and Southside Avenue Church are engaged in *processes* of learning, spiritual growth, and change. Andrea can only adopt a stance of faith toward future possibilities and toward her own and the congregation's potential as gospel proclaimers.

Embracing these truths *in her actions* as pastoral leader creates a significant challenge. The challenge is personal and internal. The challenge is also spiritual.

What is this challenge? To guide congregations toward health, toward transforming work, pastoral leaders have to face their own fears and anxieties *about their leadership identities*. For example, Andrea often asks a question that points to one of her leadership anxieties: "Is Southside Avenue really a place where I can nurture my own voice and identity as minister?"

Andrea sometimes fears losing her unique pastoral and spiritual voice. Could this fear be linked to another one? Andrea admitted as much to a friend. Over coffee, she heard herself announcing what may be her worst fear: "What will it say about me as a pastor if my church dies?" These questions are less about Southside Avenue Church than they are about Andrea's self-identity and confidence.

A goal for Andrea is to find healthy ways to face her fears and move through them in a stance of faith, courage, and hope. She can do this self work in a variety of venues such as spiritual formation, counseling, coaching, or peer dialogue groups. What is important is for Andrea to lessen her personal and spiritual anxiety *as a leader.*

A pastoral leader's personal, internal, and spiritual health is vital to congregational health. Pastoral leaders are charged with working with congregations to shape containers or vessels where congregants can do the formational work they need to do. For those vessels to be safe and transformative, they cannot be formed from the clay of a leader's personal fears about leadership or success.

As pastoral leaders build relationships, prepare sermons, administrate programs, or provide pastoral care, they must continually ask themselves important questions:

- Does my response in this situation (death of a church member, budgetary decision making, conflict management) come from my fear and anxiety or out of my sense of God's grace?
- Does this sermon reflect a vision colored more by my anxiety or by my engagement with a prophetic consciousness?
- Are my strategies in this instance fueled by personal anxieties and agendas or by the questions this congregation is striving to imagine and live?

One other question overarches these and can guide a pastoral leader's leadership decisions and his or her vocational journey.

- Does "who I am" match "what I do"?

Pastoral health is not a product. Like ministry, pastoral health is an ongoing, lifelong process. But disciplined commitment to the process does shape leaders in important ways. First, pastoral leaders who wrestle with the above questions develop a capacity to listen intently to what other people are saying. They learn to recognize when they are listening through the narrow filter of their anxieties. They also are equipped to nurture the related spiritual discipline of listening to God. In other words, they develop skills of *ministry as proclamation.*

Second, pastoral leaders who wrestle with questions of self-awareness develop a capacity to articulate what they hear in clear and memorable ways. They become able to recognize, name, and value their own voices, God's voice, the voices of culture, and the voices of others. They develop skills of *ministry as formation.*

Third, pastoral leaders who wrestle with questions of personal and ministerial identity facilitate similar work in congregations. Can we imagine the outcome if congregations engaged the above leadership identity questions?

Consider the following:

- Does our congregational response in this situation (changing neighborhood, budgetary decision making, conflict management) come from our fears and anxieties or out of our sense of God's grace?
- Do our congregational storytelling and biblical interpretation reflect a vision colored more by our anxieties or by our engagement with God's Spirit?
- Are our congregational strategies in the face of a changing neighborhood fueled by our anxieties and fears or by the questions God is calling this congregation in this time and place to imagine and live?
- Does "who we are" match "what we do"?

Once a healthy sense of congregational identity begins to emerge out of these questions, a voice and vision for the future will also emerge. The pastoral leader and congregation can embody *ministry as transformation*.

Again, the role of pastoral leader is vital as congregations struggle to put voice, clay, and fiber together. Integration is difficult work. But the pastoral leader does not bear alone the burden of creating an integrated vision. Rather, she or he must be able to tease out and name shared values present in congregational stories, actions, and insights. Pastoral leaders must develop the capacity to articulate over and over again the congregational voice, identity, and vision that emerge as congregations take up transforming gospel work.

On the heels of the anniversary celebration, Andrea guided the church council through a four-week leadership study. They spent the third session of the study brainstorming. "We need to get connected with other churches," one council leader insisted. "Some churches around here have really found an answer to multicultural ministry. Maybe they can advise us."

Andrea responded: "What kinds of connections with other churches do you think will be healthiest for us?" Ideas began to flow. Some of them surfaced in the form of springboard stories about other church partnerships tried in the past. Some surfaced as stories about congregational partnerships in the surrounding community. Several of these partnerships seem to be addressing needs and issues in local Hispanic communities.

Again, Andrea responded: "What could we contribute to a partnership like that?" Thus, the leadership study progressed. Discussion that day concluded with a request from one council member: "Maybe we can take some time at our next meeting to walk through the neighborhood like you have done. I haven't really paid enough attention to what's springing up around here."

"Can these bones live?" Irony is woven into the fact that God is the "asker" and not the "answerer" of this question in Ezekiel. Ezekiel also resists answering the question. Instead, what unfolds on the valley floor is a dance. God infuses the bones with Spirit-breath. God forms the bones with sinews and flesh. God covers the bones with skin. The bones clatter up out of the dust of the valley, dancing with new life.

The next time Andrea stepped out of the church doors into the Southside Avenue soundscape, she was not alone. Five church council members walked down the street and into the neighborhood with her. Three were eager; one was skeptical but willing; a fifth was apathetic but joined the others anyway.

They stopped for lunch at a new restaurant, Taco Riendo. One council member asked the waiter, "What does 'Taco Riendo' mean?" The accent was thick, but the words in response were clear, "Laughing Taco." They all laughed.

Andrea glanced out the window. Three teenage boys walked down the street toward Southside Avenue Church while bouncing a basketball. She looked around the table at her church leaders. She heard the Spanish conversation between waiters and cooks in the kitchen. The question came to her again: "Can these bones live?"

Andrea knows she cannot give an answer to this question. But for the first time the question is not quite as frightening.

Notes

Introduction

1. Ronald C. Williams, *Serving God with Style: Unleashing Servant Potential* (Bethesda, Md.: The Alban Institute, 2002), 1-2. Williams writes that "models developed in secular organizations" are not closely enough related to the core work of congregational life that deals with "nurturing of people in a growing knowledge of faith."

Chapter 1: Do You Hear What I Hear?

1. Mary Lin Hudson and Mary Donovan Turner *Saved from Silence: Finding Women's Voice in Preaching* (St. Louis: Chalice, 1999), 19-33. Turner and Hudson examine texts in the Hebrew Scriptures that depict God as one who has a voice. See also Dale Patrick, *The Rendering of God in the Old Testament* (Philadelphia: Fortress, 1981).

2. R. Murray Schafer, *The Tuning of the World* (New York: Knopf, 1977), 276.

3. Hudson and Turner, *Saved from Silence*, 47, 49.

4. Karen Baker-Fletcher, " 'Soprano Obligato': The Voices of Black Women and American Conflict in the Thought of Anna Julia Cooper," in *A Troubling in My Soul*, ed. Emilie M. Townes (Maryknoll, N.Y.: Orbis, 1993), 172-85.

5. Kristin Linklater, *Freeing the Natural Voice* (New York: Drama Book Specialists, 1976), 1.

6. Stephen H. Webb, *The Divine Voice: Christian Proclamation and the Theology of Sound* (Grand Rapids: Brazos, 2004), 62.

7. Linklater, *Freeing the Natural Voice*, 1-2. Linklater focuses on the interconnectedness of voice and body. See also Turner and Hudson, *Saved from Silence*, 8-10. Hudson and Turner argue that authentic speaking involves a "totality of being."

8. John Huizinga, *The Waning of the Middle Ages: A Study of the Forms of Life, Thought and Art in France and the Netherlands in the XIVth and XVth Centuries* (1924; repr., London: Edward Arnold, 1970), 2-3. Huizinga writes of the historical presence of church bells and their role in marking important moments of communal life.

9. Larry Fine, *The Piano Book: Buying and Owning a New or Used Piano*, 4th ed. (Boston: Brookside, 2001), 3.

10. Karen Tracy, *Everyday Talk: Building and Reflecting Identities* (New York: Guilford, 2002). Tracy uses the term *everyday talk* to refer to people's daily communications, and argues that everyday talk reflects and builds personal identity.

11. *The New Webster's Encyclopedia of Dictionaries* (Baltimore: Ottenheimer Publishers, 1992), s.v. "proclamation."

12. J. I. Rodale, *The Synonym Finder,* revised by Laurence Urdang and Nancy LaRoche (New York: Warner, 1986), s.v. "proclaim."

13. Webb, *The Divine Voice,* 166.

14. Schafer, *The Tuning of the World,* 10.

15. See Donald E. Messer, *Contemporary Images of Christian Ministry* (Nashville: Abingdon, 1989), 164.

16. See Webb, *The Divine Voice,* 13.

17. John L. Locke, *The De-Voicing of Society: Why We Don't Talk to Each Other Anymore* (New York: Simon & Schuster, 1998), 18-19.

18. Tom Beaudoin, *Virtual Faith: The Irreverent Spiritual Quest of Generation X* (San Francisco: Jossey-Bass, 1998). Beaudoin discusses the influence of the Internet and virtual reality on the faith development of persons in the cohort called Generation X.

19. Brad R. Braxton, *Preaching Paul* (Nashville: Abingdon, 2004), 27.

20. William A. Graham, *Beyond the Written Word: Oral Aspects of Scripture in the History of Religion* (New York: Cambridge University Press, 1987), 120.

21. Webb, *The Divine Voice,* 207.

22. See Gordon Lathrop, *Holy Things: A Liturgical Theology* (Minneapolis: Fortress, 1993), 9.

23. Rebecca Chopp, *The Power to Speak: Feminism, Language, God* (New York: Crossroad, 1989), 53.

24. Walter Brueggemann, *Theology of the Old Testament: Testimony, Dispute, Advocacy* (Philadelphia: Augsburg, 1997), 743. Brueggemann writes that discerning what is and is not "true speech" about God or from God is the work of "a community with an intentional speech practice of its own."

25. Letty Russell, *Church in the Round: Feminist Interpretation of the Church* (Louisville: Westminster John Knox, 1993), 17. Russell frames her work on the church using the metaphor of a table. She speaks about the "round table" as "a symbol of hospitality and a metaphor for gathering for sharing and dialogue."

26. See Lucy Atkinson Rose, *Sharing the Word: Preaching in the Roundtable Church* (Louisville: Westminster John Knox, 1997), 121-31.

27. John S. McClure, *Other-Wise Preaching: A Postmodern Ethic for Homiletics* (St. Louis: Chalice, 2001), 59.

28. Ibid, 134.

29. Lathrop, *Holy Things,* 98-99.

Chapter 2: Sound Approaches to Ministry as Proclamation

1. Hildegard Westerkamp, "The World Soundscape Project," *The Soundscape* Newsletter 1 (August 1991), http://interact.uoregon.edu/MediaLit/WFAE/news_letter/01.html (accessed August 8, 2005).

2. Hildegard Westerkamp, "Soundwalking," *Sound Heritage* 3, no. 4 (1974): 18.

3. Carol Gilligan, *In a Different Voice: Psychological Theory and Women's Development* (Cambridge, Mass.: Harvard University Press, 1993), xvi.

4. Stephen Zades and Jane Stephens, *Mad Dogs, Dreamers, and Sages: Growth in the Age of Ideas* (Elounda, 2003), 71.

5. Ibid., 72.

6. Ibid., 69.

7. Robert P. Roth, *Story and Reality: An Essay on Truth* (Grand Rapids: Eerdmans, 1973), 73-74.

8. Sandra Cisneros, "Woman Hollering Creek," in *Woman Hollering Creek and Other Stories* (New York: Random House, 1991), 48.

9. Arthur Plotnik, *The Elements of Expression: Putting Thoughts into Words* (New York: Henry Holt, 1996), 63.

10. Ibid.

11. Brad R. Braxton, *Preaching Paul* (Nashville: Abingdon, 2004), 33.

12. Plotnik, *The Elements of Expression*, 59.

13. Ibid.

14. Gilligan, *In a Different Voice*, xxi.

Chapter 3: A God Who Makes and Forms

1. *The New Webster's Encyclopedia of Dictionaries* (Baltimore: Ottenheimer Publishers, 1992), s.v. "form."

2. Robin Hopper, *Functional Pottery: Form and Aesthetic in Pots of Purpose*, 2nd ed. (Iola, Wisc.: Krause Publications, 2000), 20.

3. Ibid., 117.

4. Ibid.

5. Sydney Walker, "Big Ideas: Understanding the Artmaking Process: Reflective Practice," in *Art Education* 57 (May 2004): 6-13.

6. Daniel Keogh, "Using Narrative to Develop Healthier, More Effective Organizations," (PhD diss., Benedictine University, 2003), 1.

7. Walter Brueggemann, *Theology of the Old Testament: Testimony, Dispute, Advocacy* (Minneapolis: Fortress, 1997), 146.

8. See Arthur Frank, *The Wounded Storyteller: Body, Illness, and Ethics* (Chicago: The University of Chicago Press, 1995), 53.

9. Ibid., 1.

10. Ibid., xiii.

11. Ibid., xii.

12. Joy Webster Barbre et al., eds., *Interpreting Women's Lives: Feminist Theory and Personal Narratives* (Bloomington: Indiana University Press, 1989), 99. Barbre et al. write that the term *model* "derived from the empirical sciences, may imply a structure to be imitated." Narrative forms are "fluid rather than fixed" in the shapes they can take.

13. Robert McAfee Brown, "My Story and 'The Story,'" *Theology Today* 32 (July 1975): 166.

14. Ibid., 170.

15. See Sallie McFague, *Speaking in Parables: A Study in Metaphor and Theology* (Philadelphia: Fortress, 1975); James Wm. McClendon Jr., *Biography as Theology: How Life Stories Can Remake Today's Theology* (Nashville: Abingdon, 1974); George W. Stroup, *The Promise of Narrative Theology: Recovering the Gospel in the Church* (Atlanta: John Knox, 1981); Robert P. Roth, *Story and Reality* (Grand Rapids: Eerdmans, 1973); John Shea, *Stories of God: An Unauthorized Biography* (Chicago: Thomas More, 1978).

16. *The New Webster's Encyclopedia of Dictionaries* (Baltimore: Ottenheimer Publishers, 1992), s.v., "canon."

17. Heather Walton, "Speaking in Signs: Narrative and Trauma in Pastoral Theology," *Scottish Journal of Healthcare Chaplaincy* 5 (2002): 2.

18. Sara Lawrence-Lightfoot, foreword to *Katie's Canon: Womanism and the Soul of the Black Community*, by Katie Cannon (New York: Continuum, 1995), 9.

19. Cannon, ibid., 68. See also Elizabeth A. Say, *Evidence on Her Own Behalf: Women's Narrative as Theological Voice* (Savage, Md.: Rowman & Littlefield, 1990), 4. Say stresses that "through our stories we come to create and understand ourselves." Like Cannon, she focuses on voices and stories not always heard in the Bible or Christian history.

20. Walton, "Speaking in Signs," 3.

21. Cannon, *Katie's Canon*, 15.

Chapter 4: In God's House Are Many Rooms

1. See Gerard Loughlin, *Telling God's Story: Bible, Church, and Narrative Theology* (Cambridge: Cambridge University Press, 1996), 224-26.

2. Ibid, 224.

3. *The New Webster's Encyclopedia of Dictionaries* (Baltimore: Ottenheimer Publishers, 1992), s.v. "testimony."

4. Elizabeth Conde-Frazier, "Doing Theology," *Common Ground Journal* 1 (Spring 2004), http://www.commongroundjournal.org/v01n02/v01n02w1.html#Doing (accessed November 29, 2005).

5. Margaret Ann Crain and Jack Seymour, "The Thrashing in the Night: Laity Speak about Religious Knowing," *Religious Education* 92, no. 1 (Winter 1997): 43.

6. Ibid., 38.

7. Ibid.

8. Ibid.

9. Letty M. Russell, *Church in the Round: Feminist Interpretation of the Church* (Louisville: Westminster John Knox, 1993), 173.

10. See Crain and Seymour, "The Thrashing in the Night," 41.

11. Thomas G. Long, *The Witness of Preaching* (Louisville: Westminster John Knox, 1989), 43.

12. Paraphrased from a class group project.

13. Paraphrased from a class group project.

14. Russell, *Church in the Round*, 178.

15. See Morris J. Niedenthal, "The Irony and Grammar of the Gospel," in Edmund A. Steimle, Morris J. Niedenthal, and Charles L. Rice, *Preaching the Story* (Philadelphia: Fortress, 1980), 79.

16. See Leonora Tubbs Tisdale, *Preaching as Local Theology and Folk Art* (Minneapolis: Fortress, 1997), 95.

17. Ibid.

18. See Stephen Denning, *The Springboard: How Storytelling Ignites Action in Knowledge-Era Organization* (Boston: Butterworth-Heinemann, 2001). Denning discusses at length the "springboard" function of storytelling in corporations.

19. Ibid., 112-13.

20. Ibid., 178.

21. Ibid., 188-91.

22. See David M. Boje, "Stories of the Storytelling Organization: A Postmodern Analysis

of Disney as 'Tamaraland,'" *Academy of Management Journal* 38 (August 1995): 997-1035; John Krizanc, *Tamara* (Toronto: Stoddart, 1989).

23. See David M. Boje, "What Is Tamara Play?" *Tamara: Journal of Critical Postmodern Organization Science 1*, no. 1 (2001), http://tamarajournal.com (accessed November 29, 2005).

24. David M. Boje, "Athletic Apparel Industry Is Tamara-land," *Tamara: Journal of Critical Postmodern Organization Science 1*, no. 2 (2001), http://tamarajournal.com (accessed December 1, 2005).

25. Boje, "Stories of the Storytelling Organization," 999.

26. Boje, "Editorial."

27. Boje, "Stories of the Storytelling Organization," 999.

Chapter 5: I Love to Tell the Story

1. *The New Webster's Encyclopedia of Dictionaries* (Baltimore: Ottenheimer Publishers, 1992), s.v. "curiosity."

2. David Beswick, "An Introduction to the Study of Curiosity" (lecture, St. Hilda's College, The University of Melbourne, May 10, 2000), http://www.beswick.info/psychres/curiosityintro.htm (accessed December 5, 2005). See also David Beswick, "From Curiosity to Identity" (lecture, St. Hilda's College, The University of Melbourne, November 3, 2004, http://www.beswick.info/psychres/curiosityIdentity.htm (accessed December 5, 2005).

3. Ibid.

4. *The New International Webster's Pocket Dictionary of the English Language* (Naples, Fl.: Trident Press International, 1997), s.v. "curiosity."

5. See James V. Schall, "From Curiosity to Pride: On the Experience of Our Own Existence," in *Faith and the Life of the Intellect*, ed. Curtis L. Hancock and Brendan Sweetman (Washington, D.C.: Catholic University Press of America), 191.

6. Rachel Carson, *The Sense of Wonder* (New York: Harper & Row, 1956), 42-43.

7. *The Oxford American College Dictionary* (New York: Oxford University Press, 2001), s.v. "wonder."

8. Ibid.

9. Ibid., s.v. "awe."

10. Abraham Joshua Heschel, *I Asked for Wonder: A Spiritual Anthology*, ed. Samuel H. Dresner (New York: Crossroad, 1983), 3.

11. See Beswick, "An Introduction to the Study of Curiosity."

12. Charles M. Schulz, *Dogs Don't Eat Dessert* (New York: Topper, 1987), quoted in James V. Schall, "From Curiosity to Pride: On the Experience of Our Own Existence," in *Faith and the Life of the Intellect*, ed. Curtis L. Hancock and Brendan Sweetman (Washington: The Catholic University of America Press, 2003), 196-97.

13. Dorothy Leeds, *The 7 Powers of Questions: Secrets to Successful Communication in Life and at Work* (New York: A Perigee Book, The Berkeley Publishing Group, Penguin Putnam, 2000), 9. See also Susan J. Wolfson, *The Questioning Presence: Wordsworth, Keats, and the Interrogative Mode in Romantic Poetry* (Ithaca, N.Y.: Cornell University Press, 1986).

14. Ibid.

15. Patricia O'Connell Killen and John de Beer, *The Art of Theological Reflection* (New York: Crossroad, 1994), viii.

16. Lenora Tubbs Tisdale, *Preaching as Local Theology and Folk Art* (Minneapolis: Fortress, 1997), 61.

17. James P. Spradley, *The Ethnographic Interview* (Orlando: Harcourt Brace Jovanovich, 1979), 3.

18. E. H. Schein, *The Corporate Culture Survival Guide: Sense and Nonsense Aboout Culture Change* (San Francisco: Jossey-Bass, 1999), 15-20.

19. Tisdale, *Preaching as Local Theology and Folk Art,* 67.

20. Ibid.

21. Ibid.

22. *Merriam-Webster Online Dictionary,* s.v. "fluent," http://www.m-w.com/dictionary/fluent (accessed December 5, 2005).

23. Marina Umaschi Bers, "Kaleidostories: Sharing Stories across the World in a Constructionist Virtual Community for Learning," *Convergence: The Journal of Research into New Media Technologies* (2003), http://www.ase.tufts.edu/devtech/Bers-kaleidostories03.doc (accessed November 20, 2005).

24. Ibid.

25. Alice Morgan, *What Is Narrative Therapy? An Easy-to-Read Introduction* (Adelaide: Dulwich Centre Publications, 2000), http://www.dulwichcentre.com.au/alicearticle.html (accessed June 21, 2005).

26. See Terrence E. Deal and Allan A. Kennedy, *Corporate Cultures: The Rites and Rituals of Corporate Life* (Reading, Mass.: Addison-Wesley, 1982).

27. See Morgan, *What Is Narrative Therapy?*

28. Stephen Denning, *The Springboard: How Storytelling Ignites Action in Knowledge-Era Organizations* (Boston, Mass.: Butterworth-Heinemann, 2001), 82-84.

29. See Jackson Carroll, *As One with Authority: Reflective Leadership in Ministry* (Louisville: Westminster John Knox, 1991).

Chapter 6: Transforming Congregations

1. Deborah Chandler, *Learning to Weave* (Loveland, Colo.: Interweave, 1995), 14.

2. Ola I. Harrison, "Restless Weaver," in *Chalice Hymnal* (Atlanta: Chalice, 2002), 658.

3. Christine Smith, *Weaving the Sermon: Preaching in a Feminist Perspective* (Louisville: Westminster John Knox, 1989), 15.

4. Ibid., 18.

5. The Center for Congregational Health, Inc., in Winston-Salem, North Carolina, provides resources for congregational health. See http://www.healthychurch.org.

6. Smith, *Weaving the Sermon,* 21.

7. Howard Thurman, *Jesus and the Disinherited* (Boston: Beacon, 1976), 11.

8. See Jacques Matthey, "Luke 4:16-30—The Spirit's Mission Manifesto—Jesus' Hermeneutics—and Luke's Editorial," *International Review of Mission* 89 (January 2000): 3-11.

9. Abraham J. Heschel, *The Prophets* (New York: Harper & Row, 1962), 26.

10. Thurman, 11.

11. Heschel, 26.

12. See John P. Kotter, *Leading Change* (Boston: Harvard Business School Press, 1996).

13. Jim Wallis, *God's Politics: Why the Right Gets It Wrong and the Left Doesn't Get It* (San Francisco: HarperSanFrancisco, 2005), 7.

14. *Merriam-Webster Online Dictionary*, s.v. "transform," http://www.m-w.com/dictionary/ fluent (accessed December 5, 2005).

15. *Merriam-Webster Online Dictionary*, s.v. "change," http://www.m-w.com/dictionary/ fluent (accessed December 5, 2005).

16. Stephen R. Covey, *Principle-Centered Leadership* (New York: Free, 1990), 18.

17. Ibid.

18. Thurman, 89.

19. See Nancy Ammerman, *Congregation and Community* (Rutgers, N.J.: Rutgers University Press, 1997). In this book, Ammerman explores the public role of congregations.

20. See *Merriam-Webster Online Dictionary*, s.v. "vocation," http://www.m-w.com/dictionary/ fluent (accessed December 5, 2005).

21. See William May, *Beleaguered Rulers: The Public Obligation of the Professional* (Louisville: Westminster John Knox, 2001), 213-15.

22. Ibid., 215.

23. Thurman, 111-12.

Chapter 7: Imaginative Questions

1. Yvette Melanson with Claire Safran, *Looking for Lost Bird: A Jewish Woman Discovers Her Navajo Roots* (New York: Perennial, 2003), 144-45.

2. See Lyle Schaller, *The Interventionist: A Conceptual Framework and Questions for Parish Consultants, Intentional Interim Ministers, Church Champions, Pastors Considering a New Call, Denominational Executives, the Recently Arrived Pastor, Counselors, and Other Intentional Interventionists in Congregational Life* (Nashville: Abingdon, 1997).

3. Ibid., 14.

4. Ibid, 15.

5. Ibid., 24.

6. Russell Ackoff, "The Future of Operational Research Is Past," *Journal of Operational Research Society* 30 (1979): 93-104.

7. Jill Crainshaw, *Wise and Discerning Hearts: An Introduction to Wisdom Liturgical Theology* (Collegeville, Minn.: The Liturgical Press, 2000), 72. See also Donald Schon, *The Reflective Practitioner: How Professionals Think in Action* (San Francisco: Basic, 1983).

8. Steven R. Covey, *Principle-Centered Leadership* (New York: Free, 1990), 158-59.

9. Miroslav Volf, *Work in the Spirit: Toward a Theology of Work* (Eugene, Oreg.: Wipf and Stock, 1991). See also Catherine M. Wallace, *Selling Ourselves Short: Why We Struggle to Earn a Living and Have a Life* (Grand Rapids: Brazos, 2003); and R. Paul Stevens, *The Other Six Days: Vocation, Work, and Ministry in Biblical Perspective* (Grand Rapids: Eerdmans, 1999).

10. Matthew Fox, *The Reinvention of Work: A New Vision of Livelihood for Our Time* (San Francisco: HarperSanFrancisco, 1994), 1.

11. Ibid., 257.

12. Ibid., 309.

Bibliography

Ackhoff, Russell. "The Future of Operational Research Is Past." *Journal of Operational Research Society* 30 (1979): 93-104.

Ammerman, Nancy Tatom, with Arthur E. Farnsley II et al. *Congregation and Community.* New Brunswick, N.J.: Rutgers University Press, 1997.

Baker-Fletcher, Karen. "'Soprano Obligato': The Voices of Black Women and American Conflict in the Thought of Anna Julia Cooper." In *A Troubling in My Soul: Womanist Perspectives on Evil and Suffering,* edited by Emilie M. Townes, 172-85. Maryknoll, N.Y.: Orbis, 1993.

Barbre, Joy Webster, et al., eds. *Interpreting Women's Lives: Feminist Theory and Personal Narratives.* Bloomington: Indiana University Press, 1989.

Bausch, William J. *Storytelling: Imagination and Faith.* Mystic, Conn.: Twenty-Third Publications, 1984.

Beaudoin, Tom. *Virtual Faith: The Irreverent Spiritual Quest of Generation X.* San Francisco: Jossey-Bass, 1998.

Bers, Marina Umaschi. "Kaleidostories: Sharing Stories across the World in a Constructionist Virtual Community for Learning." *Convergence: The Journal of Research into New Media Technologies* 9(2), 2003. http://www.ase.tufts.edu/devtech/Bers-kaleidostories03.doc. (accessed November 20, 2005).

Beswick, David. "An Introduction to the Study of Curiosity." Lecture, St. Hilda's College, The University of Melbourne, May 10, 2000. http://www.beswick.info/psychres/curiosityintro.htm (accessed December 5, 2005).

_____. "From Curiosity to Identity." Lecture, St. Hilda's College, The University of Melbourne, November 3, 2004. http://www.beswick.info/psychres/curiosityIdentity.htm (accessed December 5, 2005).

Boadt, Lawrence. *Reading the Old Testament: An Introduction.* New York: Paulist, 1984.

Boje, David M. "Athletic Apparel Industry Is Tamara-land." *Tamara: Journal of Critical Postmodern Organization Science* 1 (2001): 6-19.

_____. "Stories of the Storytelling Organization: A Postmodern Analysis of Disney as 'Tamara-Land.'" *Academy of Management Journal* 38 (August 1995): 997-1035.

_____. "What Is Tamara the Play?" Copyright (2000) by the TAMARA Website, http://www.peaceaware.com/tamara/whatistamara.htm (accessed November 18, 2005).

Braxton, Brad. *Preaching Paul.* Nashville: Abingdon, 2004.

Brown, Robert McAfee. "My Story and 'The Story.'" *Theology Today* 32 (July 1975): 166-73.

Brueggemann, Walter. *Theology of the Old Testament: Testimony, Dispute, Advocacy.* Minneapolis: Augsburg Fortress, 1997.

Cannon, Katie Geneva. *Katie's Canon: Womanism and the Soul of the Black Community.* New York: Continuum, 1995.

Carroll, Jackson W. *As One with Authority: Reflective Leadership in Ministry.* Louisville: Westminster John Knox, 1991.

Carson, Rachel. *The Sense of Wonder.* New York: Harper & Row, 1956.

Chandler, Deborah. *Learning to Weave.* Loveland, Colo.: Interweave, 1995.

Chopp, Rebecca. *The Power to Speak: Feminism, Language, God.* New York: Crossroad, 1989.

Cisneros, Sandra. *Woman Hollering Creek and Other Stories.* New York: Random House, 1991.

Covey, Stephen R. *Principle-Centered Leadership.* New York: Free, 1990.

Crain, Margaret Ann, and Jack Seymour. "'Thrashing in the Night': Laity Speak about Religious Knowing." *Religious Education* 92 (Winter 1997): 38-53.

Crainshaw, Jill. *Wise and Discerning Hearts: An Introduction to Wisdom Liturgical Theology.* Collegeville, Minn.: The Liturgical Press, 2000.

Crossan, John Dominic. *The Dark Interval: Towards a Theology of Story.* Sonoma, Calif.: Polebridge, 1988.

Dawkins, Richard. *Unweaving the Rainbow: Science, Delusion and the Appetite for Wonder.* Boston: Houghton Mifflin, 1998.

Deal, Terrence E., and Allan A. Kennedy. *Corporate Cultures: The Rites and Rituals of Corporate Life.* Reading, Mass.: Addison-Wesley, 1982.

Denning, Stephen. *The Springboard: How Storytelling Ignites Action in Knowledge-Era Organizations.* Boston: Butterworth-Heinemann, 2001.

Fine, Larry. *The Piano Book: Buying and Owning a New or Used Piano,* 4th ed. With foreword by Keith Jarrett. Boston: Brookside, 2001.

Fox, Matthew. *The Reinvention of Work: A New Vision of Livelihood for Our Time.* San Francisco: HarperSanFrancisco, 1994.

Frank, Arthur W. *The Wounded Storyteller: Body, Illness, and Ethics.* Chicago: University of Chicago Press, 1995.

Galindo, Israel. *The Hidden Lives of Congregations: Understanding Congregational Dynamics.* Herndon, Va.: The Alban Institute, 2004.

Gallelli, Eugene Vincent. "The Implications of Stories and Storytelling on Leadership Behavior." Ed.D., diss., East Carolina University, 2004.

Geertz, Clifford. "Thick Description: Toward an Interpretive Theory of Culture." In *The Interpretation of Cultures: Selected Essays,* 3-30. New York: Basic, 1973.

Gilligan, Carol. *In a Different Voice: Psychological Theory and Women's Development.* Cambridge, Mass.: Harvard University Press, 1993.

Graham, William A. *Beyond the Written Word: Oral Aspects of Scripture in the History of Religion.* New York: Cambridge University Press, 1987.

Haers, J., and P. de Mey. *Theology and Conversation: Towards a Relational Theology.* Leuven: Leuven University Press, 2003.

Harrison, Ola I. "Restless Weaver," in *Chalice Hymnal.* Atlanta: Chalice Press, 2002, no. 658.

Herrington, Jim, Mike Bonem, and James H. Furr. *Leading Congregational Change: A Practical Guide for the Tranformational Journey.* San Francisco: Jossey-Bass, 2000.

Heschel, Abraham Joshua. *I Asked for Wonder: A Spiritual Anthology*. Edited by Samuel H. Dresner. New York: Crossroad, 1983.

Heschel, Abraham J. *Man Is Not Alone*. New York: Farrar, Straus and Giroux, 1951.

———. *The Prophets*. New York: Harper & Row, 1962.

Hopewell, James. *Congregations: Stories and Structures*. Philadelphia: Fortress, 1987.

Hopper, Robin. *Functional Pottery: Form and Aesthetic in Pots of Purpose*, 2nd ed. Iola, Wisc.: Krause Publications, 2000.

Hudson, Mary Lin and Mary Donovan Turner. *Saved from Silence: Finding Women's Voice in Preaching*. St. Louis: Chalice, 1999.

Huizinga, J. *The Waning of the Middle Ages: A Study of the Forms of Life, Thought and Art in France and the Netherlands in the XIVth and XVth Centuries*. London: Edward Arnold, 1924.

Jarl, Ann-Cathrin. *In Justice: Women and Global Economics*. Minneapolis: Fortress, 2003.

Johnson, Luke Timothy. *Scripture and Discernment: Decision Making in the Church*. Revised and expanded edition. Nashville: Abingdon, 1996.

Keogh, Daniel. "Using Narrative to Develop Healthier, More Effective Organizations." Ph.D. diss., Benedictine University, 2003.

Killen, Patricia O'Connell, and John de Beer. *The Art of Theological Reflection*. New York: Crossroad, 1994.

Kinast, Robert L. *Let Ministry Teach: A Guide to Theological Reflection*. Collegeville, Minn.: Liturgical Press, 1996.

Kotter, John P. *Leading Change*. Boston: Harvard Business School Press, 1996.

Kouzes, James M., and Barry Z. Posner, eds. *Christian Reflections on the Leadership Challenge*. San Francisco: Jossey-Bass, 2004.

Lathrop, Gordon. *Holy Things: A Liturgical Theology*. Minneapolis: Fortress, 1993.

Leeds, Dorothy. *The 7 Powers of Questions: Secrets to Successful Communication in Life and at Work*. New York: Penguin Putnam, 2000.

Levertov, Denise. "Making Peace." In *Selected Poems*, ed. Paul A. Lacey, 150. New York: New Directions, 2002.

Linklater, Kristin. *Freeing the Natural Voice*. New York: Drama Books Specialists, 1976.

Locke, John L. *The De-Voicing of Society: Why We Don't Talk to Each Other Anymore*. New York: Simon & Schuster, 1998.

Long, Thomas G. *The Witness of Preaching*. Louisville: Westminster John Knox, 1989.

Loughlin, Gerard. *Telling God's Story: Bible, Church, and Narrative Theology*. Cambridge: Cambridge University Press, 1996.

McCarthy, John Francis. "Short Stories and Tall Tales at Work: Organizational Storytelling as a Leadership Conduit during Turbulent Times." D.B.A. diss., Boston University, 2002.

McClendon, James Wm. Jr. *Biography as Theology: How Life Stories Can Remake Today's Theology*. Nashville: Abingdon, 1974.

McFague, Sallie. *Metaphorical Theology: Models of God in Religious Language*. Philadelphia: Fortress, 1982.

———. *Speaking in Parables: A Study in Metaphor and Theology*. Philadelphia: Fortress, 1975.

Maguire, Jack. *The Power of Personal Storytelling: Spinning Tales to Connect with Others*. New York: Jeremy P. Tarcher, 1998.

Matthey, Jacques. "Luke 4:16-30—The Spirit's Mission Manifesto—Jesus'

Hermeneutics—and Luke's Editorial." *International Review of Mission* 89 (January 2000): 3-11.

May, William. *Beleaguered Rulers: The Public Obligation of the Professional*. Louisville: Westminster John Knox, 2001.

Melanson, Yvette, and Claire Safran. *Looking for Lost Bird: A Jewish Woman Discovers Her Navajo Roots*. New York: Perennial, 2003.

Messer, Donald E. *Contemporary Images of Christian Ministry*. Nashville: Abingdon, 1989.

Morgan, Alice. *What Is Narrative Therapy: An Easy-to-Read Introduction*. Adelaide: Dulwich Centre Publications, 2000, http://www.dulwichcentre.com.au/alicearticle.html (accessed June 21, 2005).

Morrison, Toni. *Beloved: A Novel*. New York: Plume, 1988.

Nelson, William R. *Ministry Formation for Effective Leadership*. Nashville: Abingdon, 1988.

Nolde, Kendra. "Evangelizing Declining Congregations in Changing Communities through Narrative Preaching." D.Min. diss., Aquinas Institute of Theology, 2001.

Oliver, Mary. "The Summer Day." In *New and Selected Poems*, 94. Boston: Beacon, 1992. Originally published in 1990 as *House of Light* by Beacon Press, 1990.

Patrick, Dale. *The Rendering of God in the Old Testament*. Philadelphia: Fortress, 1981.

Pederson, Ann. *God, Creation, and All That Jazz: A Process of Composition and Improvisation*. St. Louis: Chalice, 2001.

Personal Narratives Group. "Forms That Transform." In *Interpreting Women's Lives: Feminist Theory and Personal Narratives*, edited by Personal Narratives Group, 99-102. Bloomington: Indiana University Press, 1989.

Piepenburg, Robert. *The Spirit of Clay: A Classic Guide to Ceramics*. Farmington Hills, Mich.: Pebble, 1998.

Plotnik, Arthur. *The Elements of Expression: Putting Thoughts into Words*. New York: Henry Holt, 1996.

Rodale, J. I. *The Synonym Finder*. Revised by Laurence Urdang and Nancy LaRoche. New York: Warner, 1986.

Rose, Lucy Atkinson. *Sharing the Word: Preaching in the Roundtable Church*. Louisville: Westminster John Knox, 1997.

Roth, Robert P. *Story and Reality: An Essay on Truth*. Grand Rapids: Eerdmans, 1973.

Russell, Letty. *Church in the Round: Feminist Interpretation of the Church*. Louisville: Westminster John Knox, 1993.

Say, Elizabeth A. *Evidence on Her Own Behalf: Women's Narrative as Theological Voice*. Savage, Md.: Rowman & Littlefield, 1990.

Schafer, R. Murray. *The Tuning of the World*. New York: Knopf, 1977.

Schall, James V. "From Curiosity to Pride: On the Experiences of Our Own Existence." In *Faith and the Life of the Intellect*, edited by Curtis L. Hancock and Brendan Sweetman, 187-209. The Catholic University of America Press, 2003.

Schaller, Lyle. *The Interventionist*. Nashville: Abingdon Press, 2002.

Schank, Roger C. *Tell Me a Story: Narrative and Intelligence*. Evanston, Ill.: Northwestern University Press, 1995. Originally published in 1990 as *Tell Me a Story: A New Look at Real and Artificial Memory* by Scribner.

Schein, Edgar H. *The Corporate Culture Survival Guide: Sense and Nonsense about Culture Change*. San Francisco: Jossey-Bass, 1999.

Schon, Donald. *The Reflective Practitioner: How Professionals Think in Action*. San Francisco: Basic, 1983.

Schulz, Charles M. *Dogs Don't Eat Dessert*. New York: Topper, 1987.

Schüssler Fiorenza, Elisabeth. *Wisdom Ways: Introducing Feminist Biblical Interpretation*. Maryknoll, N.Y.: Orbis, 2001.

Shea, John. *Stories of God: An Unauthorized Biography*. Chicago: Thomas More, 1978.

Simmons, Annette. *A Safe Place for Dangerous Truths: Using Dialogue to Overcome Fear and Distrust at Work*. New York: AMACOM, 1999.

Smith, Christine M. *Weaving the Sermon: Preaching in a Feminist Perspective*. Louisville: Westminster John Knox, 1989.

Spradley, James P. *The Ethnographic Interview*. Fort Worth: Harcourt Brace Jovanovich, 1979.

Steimle, Edmund A., Morris J. Niedenthal, and Charles L. Rice. *Preaching the Story*. Philadelphia: Fortress, 1980.

Stepto, Robert B. *From Behind the Veil: A Study of Afro-American Narrative*. Urbana: University of Illinois Press, 1991.

Stevens, R. Paul. *The Other Six Days: Vocation, Work, and Ministry in Biblical Perspective*. Grand Rapids: Eerdmans, 1999.

Stroup, George W. *The Promise of Narrative Theology: Recovering the Gospel in the Church*. Atlanta: John Knox, 1981.

Thurman, Howard. *Jesus and the Disinherited*. New York: Abingdon-Cokesbury, 1949. Reprinted with foreword by Vincent Harding. Boston: Beacon, 1996.

Tisdale, Leonora Tubbs. *Preaching as Local Theology and Folk Art*. Minneapolis: Fortress, 1997.

Tracy, Karen. *Everyday Talk: Building and Reflecting Identities*. New York: Guilford, 2002.

Trible, Phyllis. *Texts of Terror: Literary-Feminist Readings of Biblical Narratives*. Overtures to Biblical Theology 13. Philadelphia: Fortress Press, 1984.

Troeger, Thomas. *Imagining a Sermon*. Nashville: Abingdon, 1990.

Volf, Miroslav. *Work in the Spirit: Toward a Theology of Work*. New York: Oxford University Press, 1991. Reprinted in 2001 by Wipf and Stock.

Walker, Sydney. "Big Ideas: Understanding the Artmaking Process: Reflective Practice." *Art Education* 57 (May 2004): 6-13.

Wallace, Catherine M. *Selling Ourselves Short: Why We Struggle to Earn a Living and Have a Life*. Grand Rapids: Brazos, 2003.

Wallis, Jim. *God's Politics: Why the Right Gets It Wrong and the Left Doesn't Get It*. San Francisco: HarperSanFrancisco, 2005.

Walton, Heather. "Speaking in Signs: Narrative and Trauma in Pastoral Theology." *Scottish Journal of Healthcare Chaplaincy* 5 (2002): 2-5.

Webb, Stephen H. *The Divine Voice: Christian Proclamation and the Theology of Sound*. Grand Rapids, Mich.: Brazos, 2004.

Westerkamp, Hildegard. "The World Soundscape Project," *The Soundscape Newsletter* 1 (August 1991). http://interact.uoregon.edu/MediaLit/WFAE/news_letter/ol.html. Internet. Accessed August 8, 2005.

_____. "Soundwalking," *Sound Heritage* 3, no. 4 (1974): 18.

Whitehead, James D., and Evelyn Eaton Whitehead. *Method in Ministry: Theological Reflection and Christian Ministry*, rev. and updated. Kansas City, Mo.: Sheed & Ward, 1995.

Williams, Ronald C. *Serving God with Style: Unleashing Servant Potential*. Bethesda, Md.: The Alban Institute, 2002.

Wolfson, Susan J. *The Questioning Presence: Wordsworth, Keats, and the Interrogative Mode in Romantic Poetry*. Ithaca, N.Y.: Cornell University Press, 1986.

Zades, Stephen, and Jane Stephens. *Mad Dogs, Dreamers, and Sages: Growth in the Age of Ideas*. Elounda, 2003.